RESCUE TAILS 2

LOVE FINDS A HOME

JULIANN BISTRANIN

GALLIVANT
PRESS

Paperback ISBN: 978-1-947894-56-3

Printed in USA

DEDICATION

To Janine Ceja, my director, who has dedicated her life to animal welfare. You are an inspiration.

To all my co-workers, fellow board members, and friends who work tirelessly, giving your time and countless hours of effort to make the lives of animals a little less lonely, stressful, and traumatic. Your compassion is remarkable.

To my husband, Mark, and my children, Kim, Melynda, and Lance, and their families, who have been such an encouragement to me.

To my dog Roper, who has never once agreed that writing is more important than a hike.

CONTENTS

FOREWORD

Julie Bistranin is my next-door neighbor. For years, I have had the pleasure of watching her walk her rescued dogs and seeing them become calmer, happier, and better companions because of her professional experience and natural ability to communicate with animals. My friends have also benefited from her remarkable talent for matching people with the perfect dog. I loved, shared, and recommended her first book, Rescue Tails, and I cannot wait for the next one in the series.

- GINNY DARVILL

I remember one of the first dogs we had as a family. He was a golden brown with a perfect white tie around his neck, soft velvety ears, and the most soulful eyes. His name was Ty, and we spent countless sun-drenched hours running through the fields that stretched around our house. Ty had his quirks. He was not fond of Mom's pancakes (a tragic mystery), but he never, ever missed a truck ride.

The question is, how do we find them? How do we find our pets, our dogs or cats, our best friends? Sometimes they arrive in our lives in the full bloom of youth; sometimes we are lucky enough to be there to witness the gentle end of their journey. Regardless of when they find us, or when we find them, they change us. They shift the rhythm of our days and the landscape of our hearts.

This new book Julie has written is a tribute to that impact. It shares the stories of best friends, of unforgettable, life-altering connections that only a rescue can bring.

- Kimberly Knoernschild

INTRODUCTION

According to the ASPCA, 3.9 million dogs enter shelters nationwide every year. Shelter workers have the daunting task of finding them homes where they can begin a new life. Every dog has a story and a past, but once they enter the shelter, I tried to wipe the slate clean and give them a fresh start.

I loved my job, and I loved each dog. One day, I met Scout, a German Shepherd whose owners claimed she was a trained narcotics dog. When she came into my evaluation room, I was curious to see if what they had told me was true.

"Scout," I said, "do you want to go to work?"

Her ears pricked forward, and she wagged her tail excitedly. Harnessing her up, I led her out to the shelter parking lot.

"Okay, girl, let us see if they were telling the truth," I said. "Search, Scout."

Immediately, she started smelling around each car. When she reached one of our employee's cars, she sat down. I thought at first it was just a coincidence, so I took her back indoors. I waited for about a half hour, and then, out of curiosity, I took her back outdoors.

"Search, Scout," I instructed.

Once more, she started smelling around each car, and when she reached the employee's car, she once again sat down.

"Good girl, Scout," I said.

Laughing, I now had the task of telling the employee she had been caught red-handed by one of our shelter dogs.

Our goal at the shelter is to give the dogs who come to us a second chance at life with a new home and family. Some of the dogs you will read about in my new book, such as Laura the Golden Retriever or Moose the German Shepherd, found exactly that. I think you will love each chapter because each one carries a message of hope.

These are stories of dogs given a second chance, becoming welcomed family members or going on to serve their communities in meaningful ways. When you read a book, the ending sometimes says the end. My books should be signed with the beginning, because they are stories of dogs who arrived at the Humane Society and then started a new life with new beginnings. And yes, we did find Scout a home.

A Companion for Life

That is how a dog thinks,
Loyalty is set deep,
deep in his heart.
Is it in yours, O man?
He is faithful.
Laying quietly by the door.
Listening for your footsteps.
Are you coming home?
Or have you forgotten, O man?
He seeks your love,
Adoring you with his eyes,
Placing you in his heart,
As you look down at him
Do you adore him too, O man?
He is playful,
Entertaining you, trying to make you laugh,
It is not foolishness to him,
Is it foolishness to you,
Or do you laugh, O man?
To him you are not insignificant,
You are wonderful,
Is he wonderful to you, O man?
He didn't ask for you to take ownership of him,
But you have, O man.
Do you love him?
Will you care for him as much as he cares for you,
This dog of yours,
O man?

Juliann Bistranan

CHUCK (AKA BOBBY)

WELL, this was a first. I had seen a lot of things at the shelter, but never anything like this. On a warm sunny afternoon in early November, a woman called to ask if she could bring her dog in because of an emergency in her family. We told her she could, making arrangements for her to bring him in the next day. With the appointment set, we asked her to provide us with her dog's vet records so we would not double up on vaccines and would also have a record to send with him once he was adopted.

She arrived at the appointed time with a healthy black Labrador Retriever named Chuck. We could tell he was friendly as soon as he entered the building. He greeted each of us with a wagging tail and the happy, cordial nature typical of the Labrador breed. His owner, a woman in her early sixties, also greeted us pleasantly and with an outgoing personality.

She held out her hand to shake Heather's, introducing herself as Lillian. Dressed in hiking gear from head to toe, her gray-green eyes crinkled in a smile. Under her dark blue knitted hat, her gray hair showed natural curls.

Handing us a bag of her dog's toys, his food, and blanket, she sat down to fill out the personality profile.

"I got him from a friend when he was around a year old," she told Heather.

She reached down to pat her dog's head while continuing an ongoing conversation. She wrote out the personality profile, and when she finished, she handed Heather the papers. Reaching into her pocket, she pulled out cash to pay the intake fee.

"How much did you tell me the intake fee was when I called?" she asked.

Heather told her the amount, and Lillian carefully counted out the bills, laying them on the desktop.

"Oh darn," she said, pursing her lips. "I don't have enough, and I left my purse in the car. Would you take a check, or better yet, could I pay with a credit card?"

"That will be fine," Heather replied.

Lillian put the cash back into her pocket, and once again reached down to pet her dog.

"He's been a wonderful dog," she said. "I hate to give him up, but my husband is so ill, and I don't have the time to care for Chuck properly anymore."

She wiped away a tear. "It is so hard to give him up, because he has been such a faithful friend."

Big tears were now rolling down her cheeks as she began to cry. Heather moved around the desk to comfort her, handing her a tissue.

"Chuck is young, and he will be easy to adopt out," she tried to reassure her.

When Lillian had regained her composure, Heather moved back around the desk and began typing Chuck's information.

"Lillian, did you bring Chuck's vet records?" she asked. "We will also need a copy of your driver's license."

"Oh yes, they are in my purse in the car," Lillian said, jumping up. "I will go get them. And would you like his bed also? It is so big and cumbersome, I wasn't sure you would want it."

"Yes, that would be great," Heather told her. "We like the dogs to have their familiar things from home; it helps them adjust."

Lillian left and came back agitated.

"I am so sorry," she blurted out, looking embarrassed. "I must have left the house without my purse, the vet information, and his bed. I cannot believe it!"

She paced back and forth, flustered at being so forgetful.

"My husband is having surgery tomorrow," she said, starting to cry again. "I have been so upset and forgetful lately. I feel so stupid. Would it be possible for me to bring them tomorrow after my husband's surgery?"

"Of course you can," Heather reassured her. "I will just have you sign all the papers, and we will finish the intake tomorrow. Right now, we need to know if he is current on his vaccinations and if he has been micro-chipped."

"Oh yes, he is up to date on all his vaccines, but he is not micro-chipped," Lillian replied.

She looked at Heather guiltily. "I feel so bad that I have wasted your time, and I would like to leave some cash with you this afternoon."

"No, no," Heather told her, feeling sorry for her. "We will do everything tomorrow when you come back."

"You are so kind," Lillian said, her eyes filling with tears again. "I cannot stand myself for abandoning Chuck like this."

Sobbing, she fell to the floor in front of her dog. "I am sorry, Chuck, but I have no choice," she exclaimed.

With her head on his, she hugged him close. Heather got up and moved around the desk, kneeling down beside her.

"Lillian, do you want to take him home one last night?" she suggested. "You could bring him back tomorrow."

"No, no," Lillian sobbed. "It is too hard, and I cannot bear to do it twice."

When Lillian felt ready to leave, Heather walked her out to her car. Lillian hugged her and thanked her. As she drove off, a staff member took Chuck to the dog wing to find a warm kennel for him. She left him in his kennel, surrounded by his familiar toys, food, and blanket from home.

The next afternoon, we waited for Chuck's owner to return and finish his intake. As the afternoon faded into early evening, we became concerned because Lillian had not come back. We wondered if something had gone terribly wrong with her husband's surgery. We talked it over and agreed to wait until the next day before placing a call to her.

Chuck seemed untroubled and content, charming every visitor and staff member. The following day, when we still had not heard from Lillian, Heather tried to call her, only to reach voicemail. She heard Lillian's cheerful voice asking callers to leave a number and message and promising to return calls as soon as possible.

Days three, four, five, and six went by with no word from Lillian. Still concerned, we searched the local papers for her husband's obituary. As the days passed, we decided Chuck had been abandoned. This created a new situation for us. When a dog is abandoned on our property or anywhere in the county, we must hold them for seventy-two hours or longer.

We searched the lost-dog book, placed calls to the county and city animal control officers, and asked them to check whether they had any lost or found reports matching Chuck's description. Since we had Chuck's owner's name and address, we asked animal control to perform a welfare check.

When Officer Anderson called us back, he informed us

there was no such person living at the address Lillian had given.

"We have been had," Heather blurted out.

"That woman should win an Academy Award for acting," she stormed, waving her hands in the air as if swiping away all the lies Lillian had told.

We listened empathetically to Heather's frustration.

"She seemed like such a nice person," she fumed. "I cannot believe I fell for it."

Placing her hands on her hips, she looked as if she were preparing for battle. Our director looked at her sympathetically.

"Well, at least she brought him here. She could have abandoned him somewhere out in the cold."

"It still makes me feel so gullible, like a fool," Heather said, furious. "I am losing all trust in people. She seemed so nice, while the whole time she was pulling me into her drama."

Heather slammed some papers down angrily.

"She played me like a fiddle."

We all felt sorry for Heather as she moved around the room, indignant at being so deceived. People sometimes lie when they come to the shelter and do not tell us everything they know about the animal they are bringing in, but this situation was entirely new to us. Lillian's performance was something none of the staff had ever encountered, and it stunned us all.

Meanwhile, Chuck was happy and enjoying his stay.

Three weeks after Chuck arrived at the humane society, his hold was up and he was available for adoption. We had nicknamed him Mr. Congeniality because of his agreeable and charming nature. He loved life and delighted in every meal, every walk, every play session, and every interaction with volunteers or visitors. He savored every moment of his day.

By now, he had become a favorite among the volunteers, basking in their affection. Playing in the yard was his chance to show off his ball skills. Begging for treats was his specialty—any treat would do. He had zero hesitation about reaching for a tasty morsel in a grabby sort of way. The term I would use is mouthy, because he did not hesitate to pounce when grabbing for the treat.

As people tried to keep their fingers attached to their hands, they started insisting he sit and wait before being rewarded. Teaching him to sit helped him learn patience and become gentler while taking treats.

On the morning I took him into my office to do his evaluation, he could hardly contain himself with delight at being in a new place to explore. His powerful nose sniffed at all the tantalizing aromas in the room. Working his way along the floor, he could smell every dog who had been there before him.

Noticing an abandoned toy, he lay down on the bed and tried to disengage the noisemaker inside. Squeak, squeak, squeak echoed from the chewed toy. In the middle of a squeak, he caught the scent of something more interesting. Jumping off the bed, he poked his head underneath it. His tail swished back and forth as he dug deeper.

Overcome with joy, his head popped out with a dog treat. Chomping it down, he swallowed it and then began searching for more contraband.

He was good about coming when called, and he knew the commands sit, down, roll over, shake, and stay.

I fixed a bowl of food to test him for food aggression. While I stirred it, he sat in front of me, salivating with his tail sweeping the floor in anticipation of the upcoming feast. I placed the bowl on the floor, and he sprinted forward, burying his head deep in the bowl.

"Leave it," I told him.

Lifting his head from the bowl, he backed away and sat, but his expression clearly said:

"You have got to be kidding."

I was not sure how he would react when I reached down to pick up the bowl, but he remained quiet and pleading.

"That is a good sign," I thought.

As I lifted the bowl, he drooled, never taking his longing eyes off it. Unable to resist his imploring look, I placed the bowl back down so he could finish.

The evaluation was routine, with no red flags. I knew he would do well in any home and become a wonderful family member.

When he finished eating, he spotted another toy across the room and ran to get it. Lying on his back, he held it between his front paws. Wiggling his rear end back and forth in happiness, he suddenly let out a massive stinker, filling my office with the worst smell.

"Pew!" I said. "That reeks."

I ran to the door, waving it back and forth in an attempt to dissipate the smell into the hallway.

Returning to my desk, I sat down to type his profile for the website. Chuck soon became bored with his toy and abandoned it. He walked over and sat beside me. As I typed, he swept the floor behind him with his tail, and to my amusement, every third swipe produced a toot.

Each time, he looked startled and turned his head toward his rear end. Concerned, he looked back at me with an expression that said:

"What was that?"

Laughing, I got up again to open the door and clear the odor.

I wrote on his paperwork: *He emits gas (farts). He is a very stinky kind of guy.*

Once his evaluation was complete, I picked up the microchip scanner and scanned him. The staff had already checked him, but it was part of my evaluation to verify one last time. I ran the scanner around his neck, shoulders, and down his back. I pushed it down his front legs as well, because in the past I had found microchips there.

Beep, beep, beep. The scanner sounded. I lifted it to read the numbers on the screen. Quickly, I wrote them down and texted Emmi to come to my office.

"What is up?" she asked, looking in.

"He is micro-chipped," I told her.

"You are kidding," she said, surprised.

She stepped inside and shut the door behind her. "I thought his owner said he was not micro-chipped."

"It is in his right front leg," I replied. "You know me; I find them in strange places."

I handed her the paper with the chip number.

"I will go call," she said. "That is strange. She must have forgotten."

"Did she not say a friend gave her the dog?" I said. "Maybe she did not know he was chipped."

"That is hard for me to believe. A vet clinic should have found it," Emmi replied.

She opened the door to leave but turned back, wrinkling her nose.

"What is that smell?"

"It is Chuck," I said. "He passes gas."

"Oh boy," Emmi said, waving her hand in front of her face. "Maybe we should adopt him out to someone who had Covid, and no longer has a sense of smell."

Shaking her head, she shut my door.

After returning Chuck to his kennel, I went back to my office to file his evaluation. A moment later, Emmi knocked and stepped inside, waving a piece of paper she had been writing on.

"You are not going to believe this!" she said, taking a seat. "Chuck's real name is Bobby, and he was stolen."

"What!" I exclaimed, falling back in my chair.

"Yes. He belongs to a guy named Erik."

"You mean the guy Lillian got him from?" I asked.

"No. He is the guy Lillian stole him from," she replied.

"I have got to hear this one," I said.

There was another knock on the door, and Heather came in.

"Did you hear about Chuck?"

"I was just telling her," Emmi said quickly, not wanting Heather to spill the rest before she could.

"This guy Erik," she continued, "was hiking with his puppy up by Lake Diablo in the Cascades. As he was hiking, he came upon two older women who were also on the trail. They were very friendly and told him they were hiking up to the lake and had stopped to catch their breath.

They stood on the trail talking with him and asked if they could hike alongside him for a while. He knew that because of their age, they would slow him down, but he could not say no, so they started up the trail together.

One of the women, named Lillian, loved his puppy. She told Erik she had always owned Labs. His dog, Bobby, was around six months old and had already been on several hikes with him. He wanted Bobby to be good around other people and their dogs on the trail, so he allowed people to interact with him.

They had hiked together for about a mile when Erik needed to go to the bathroom. Instead of taking his dog off the trail with him, he asked the two women if they would watch him. He went deep enough into the underbrush to have some privacy.

Suddenly, he heard one woman yelling Bobby's name. He hurried back to the trail, knowing something was wrong. When he got back, he saw only one woman. She told him Lillian had taken the leash off Bobby to play with him, and he had run up the trail.

They had called for him to come back, but he kept running. Lillian told her to wait for Erik and said she would follow the puppy and catch him.

Erik started running, calling Bobby's name. The remaining woman tried to follow, but she soon became winded. She told him to go ahead without her and that she would catch up.

He continued running up the trail, expecting that once Lillian caught Bobby, she would start back toward him. He had gone quite a way before he met some hikers coming down.

He stopped them and asked if they had seen a woman with a black Labrador puppy. They told him they had seen no one or any dogs. This stunned him because there were no side trails on that part of the route.

Concerned, he wondered if Bobby had crawled into the underbrush and if the woman had gone after him. He turned around and began making his way back down the trail, calling Bobby's name.

He had gone about a mile when he met a hiker coming up. Erik asked if he had seen a woman with a black Labrador. He said he had—there were two women with a black Lab.

He had seen them going down the trail near the parking lot. Erik began running, hoping to catch up. When he reached the lot, there were people preparing to hike. He asked a young couple if they had seen a woman with a black Lab. They had not.

But another man approached him and said he had seen two

women with a black Lab. They were in a hurry and had left. He did not remember the make of their car, but he said it was dark blue.

He said it caught his attention because before they left, they removed the dog's leash, harness, and collar and threw them into the brush.

Erik was in shock.

He crawled into the brush to retrieve Bobby's gear. He told me he has hiked the trail many times since, looking for them, but after two years he had given up hope."

I sat there astonished.

"Wow. Does he want his dog back?" I asked.

"Yes," Emmi said, smiling. "He lives in Seattle and will come up tomorrow to get him."

This was an incredible story, and I had many questions.

"Did he report to the authorities that his dog had been stolen—and to the microchip company?" I asked.

"Yes, and he put posters everywhere," Emmi said. "He called the sheriff's department, the vets in the area, left lost-dog reports at the trailheads, and contacted shelters, including ours."

I sat there stunned, trying to absorb what Emmi had just told me.

"That woman," Heather seethed. "Why would she do something so cruel? What kind of pleasure did she get out of stealing a man's dog?"

"I do not know," I said. "I am dumbfounded."

"Well, I hope someday her thievery catches up with her," Heather stormed. "The poor guy."

Another knock sounded on the door, and our director stepped inside. We sat in disbelief, discussing this new revelation about Chuck.

"I love microchips," our director said. "They solve so many mysteries."

"Well, they certainly solved this one," I said.

"We should call the paper," Heather suggested. "This is a great story, and it might expose this woman. Someone must know who she is and where she lives."

"Even if it worked, the county will most likely not do anything about it," our director replied with a frown. "We are going to return Chuck to his owner, and Erik can handle the legal end if he chooses."

We all nodded in agreement. What mattered most now was reuniting this dog with his owner.

"Oh!" Emmi said, ready to share more. "One question Erik asked was whether Bobby still passed gas. He said the dog always suffered from flatulence and had to be on a special diet."

We all laughed. Chuck's gas problem had been a frequent topic among staff and volunteers who spent time with him.

"Well, that confirms it," I said. "Chuck is definitely his dog. He has been passing gas since the day he arrived."

In this part of the story, I have to give my opinion on hiking with dogs. Being an avid hiker, I have witnessed many incidents where people put themselves, their dogs, other people, and wildlife in jeopardy on hiking trails.

When you do not have your dog leashed, you do not have control of your dog. You may think they are exceptional, well behaved, and have been through training. You trust in that training and in their ability to recall back to you. It is natural to want them to experience the freedom of hiking alongside you, leash-free.

But it only takes one incident.

An incident where your dog could get injured, lost, or worse yet, injure another person or dog on the trail. I live next to a hiking trail and have found several scared dogs on my front porch after they became lost.

I have also encountered people frightened and worried after their dogs ran into the underbrush chasing wildlife. In their frenzy, they would not come back or had possibly run far enough into the woods where they could no longer hear their owners calling for them. And why should wildlife have to fear a dog who is chasing after them?

There are also dogs who meet each other on the trail and, for reasons unknown, get into an altercation. Their owners claim they are always friendly, but on that particular day, they begin to fight. This places both owners in a position where they must break up a dogfight. Their dogs may get hurt, and they could get bitten.

One day, a woman was coming down the trail after a dog she did not know had bitten her. The owner had his dog off leash, and when she reached down to pet the dog, it reacted and bit. Who knows why the dog thought she was a threat and defended himself or his owner.

Dogs are dogs—with dog thinking.

Hiking is supposed to be an enjoyable experience until you are standing there with an empty leash in your hand, shocked that your well-trained dog just did the unthinkable.

Believe me, I know. On a lovely summer day while hiking, my well-trained dog took a dislike to an unaware hiker. He caught me completely off guard and taught me a valuable lesson. Luckily, he was on leash, and I had control.

In Erik's rare case, he lost his dog to an unstable or cruel person—someone who, for an unknown reason, committed an unthinkable act. He trusted her, and by placing his dog in the care of a stranger, she stole him.

It was probably a one-in-a-million occurrence, but it

happened. Erik lost his beloved puppy, and it all could have been prevented if he had kept control of his dog.

He got a second chance, but I wonder how many owners and their dogs do not.

The next morning arrived with the sun making a bright appearance, chasing away the November gloom. A bright red pickup pulled into the parking lot about an hour before we opened, adding a splash of color to the chilly morning. At eleven o'clock, the lights clicked on and the front door unlocked.

A young man walked in carrying a red collar, a harness, and a matching leash. He approached the front desk with a huge smile.

"Hi, I am Erik, and I am here to get my dog Bobby."

His dark curly hair stuck out from beneath a cap with an Outback logo. His voice carried an apologetic kindness as he spoke to us. He shook each of our hands, and I could feel a slight tremble—part nerves, part excitement.

Holding up the leash, collar, and harness, he smiled. "I never threw them away," he said. "Because in my heart, I always believed I would get my dog back someday."

Our director stepped out of her office to greet him.

"Erik, we are so glad to meet you—and so relieved this is a happy ending for you and Bobby," she said.

"Yes," Erik said. "I was stunned to get your call after all this time."

"Well, I am glad this is over for you, and you can stop wondering what happened to your dog," our director said warmly. "He came to us healthy and in good shape, if that is any consolation."

"I always hoped that if he was taken to a veterinarian, they would find his microchip and call me," Erik said.

The staff and volunteers introduced themselves and told

him how much they loved Bobby.

"He became one of our shelter favorites," I said. "He has such a friendly personality."

"He was always a happy dog," Erik said with a sigh. "Always ready for his next adventure. I suppose he had quite a big one."

He hesitated, then asked quietly, "Does he still pass gas? I always called him my stinky boy."

I laughed. "That part has not changed."

Emmi stepped forward.

"We need to get started with the return-to-owner process. Heather will go back and get Bobby for you."

Heather took the harness, collar, and leash and headed back to retrieve him. When we heard them coming, we stood behind Erik, all of us eager to see Bobby's reaction.

I was not sure whether Bobby would remember Erik, since he was stolen as a puppy, but animals imprint deeply. There was a real possibility he would know him.

When the door opened, Bobby trotted in happily, thinking he was going out for his morning walk.

Erik crouched down.

"Bobby!" he called.

Bobby stopped, puzzled. Something in the tone—something buried in memory—reached him.

"Bobby," Erik said again.

Bobby whimpered.

"Bobby," Erik whispered for the third time.

That was all it took.

Bobby lunged forward, yanking the leash from Heather's hand, and ran straight into Erik's open arms.

Erik gathered his wiggling dog close, hugging away two stolen years. We all cheered, clapped, and cried as they rolled on the floor together in pure joy.

"Thank you," Erik said through tears, trying to hold onto his ecstatic dog. "I cannot believe he remembers me."

"Oh, he remembers," our director said, laughing. "The look on his face said everything."

Moments like this are why we do what we do. At the shelter, we see the worst and the best of humanity—but reunions like this make all the hard days worth it.

When Erik took Bobby out to his pickup, we watched from the doorway. At the end of the driveway, he turned and waved one last time.

"This was good for my soul," Heather said softly. "I hope somehow, Lillian pays for all the misery she caused."

"I think she will," I replied, watching the truck disappear down the road.

I reflected for a moment on how things work out for people who choose kindness. As for those who break hearts and trust—life catches up with them eventually.

For Chuck—Bobby—and Erik, everything turned out the way it should.

For Lillian... what can I say? A life like hers stays in the shadows.

The bond with a true dog is as lasting as the ties of this earth will ever be.

KONRAD LORENZ

GUNNY

Gunny came to the shelter as a stray. He was found in one of the city parks where a couple was having a picnic lunch with their three children. He strolled toward them with his nose in the air, smelling their delicious food. Even though the parents told their children not to feed him, they still did, and then proceeded to play with him for the rest of the afternoon.

They ran with him, threw a ball he had found, and shrieked with delight at his funny antics. The parents listened for a person calling for their dog, hoping someone would stop by to retrieve him, but no one came.

As the afternoon waned and moved toward evening, they walked around the park asking everyone they met if they recognized the dog, but no one did. They started folding blankets and putting things back into the picnic basket so they could load the car.

Nervous about leaving the dog and not knowing what to do, they gave each other worried glances. Buckling their kids into their car seats so they could leave, the children began to cry.

Sobbing, they told their mommy and daddy they did not want to leave the dog behind.

"Mommy, no," their five-year-old cried. "He needs us."

"He is not our dog, Kit," the mom said sympathetically. "He belongs to someone else, and I am sure they will soon come to look for him."

Now all the kids were crying, and the parents looked at each other, disconcerted. The dog sat next to the car wagging his tail, waiting for an invitation to get in.

They looked down at the dog while their children wailed.

"I suppose we could take him home for the night," the mom sighed.

"I think we will have to," her husband replied. "And I will take him to a vet in the morning to see if he is micro-chipped."

So they opened the back door of the car, and the dog happily jumped inside.

"He can only stay the night, and we will look for his owners in the morning," the dad warned his children as he looked back at them from the front seat.

They drove home with happy, smiling children and the vagabond dog who had introduced himself at their picnic in the park.

True to his word, the man took the dog to a vet clinic first thing in the morning. A vet tech scanned him for a microchip but found none. He took the dog back out to his car and called animal control.

After taking a report, the officer told him to bring the dog to the Humane Society. When he got to the shelter, he told the staff what he knew about the dog and what park he had found him in.

"He is great with children," he said. "But we cannot keep him because we are renting and are not allowed to have pets."

"We will check with animal control to see if anyone has called since you talked with her," Emmi told him.

"I hate leaving him," the man said. "My kids will be heart-broken. So would you call us if you find his owner?"

"Call and check on him in a couple of days." Emmi smiled. "Hopefully by then he will be back home."

After the man left, Emmi took the dog into her office and texted me.

"Come to my office," the text read. "You have to see this brute."

When I walked through her office door, my eyes were met by an enormous dog standing next to her desk. I could tell he had Mastiff in him and was probably around eight months old. Tall and leggy, he must have weighed around ninety pounds. His coat was brindle—light brown with black stripes. He had black around his nose, which spread down around his hanging jowls. Slobber drooled out the sides of his mouth, dropping onto the floor. His wide, muscled chest had a splash of white that ran down toward his belly, and each foot had white socks. When I came in, he greeted me with a good-natured tail wag. Shaking his head, he splashed more drool around the room.

"Wow! Where did he come from?" I asked Emmi, reaching out to pet him.

"A family found him at the city park," she laughed. "They said he happily joined them for their Sunday picnic."

"He is huge!" I said, trying to dodge more flying slobber.

"They looked for his owner, but no one claimed him," Emmi said as she bent over to wipe her floor with a towel. "So they took him home for the night, and then to a vet this morning to check for a microchip."

"None?" I asked.

"No, and I just got off the phone with animal control."

She now placed the towel under his face to catch the drool.

21

"Officer Bailey looked through her reports from last weekend," Emmi said. "And there are no records of a missing Mastiff."

As I watched, the dog went into a play stance, focusing on a ball. Jumping toward it, he slapped it around the room with his huge paws. As it rolled away from him, he picked it up, and it disappeared inside his cavernous mouth.

"What are you calling him?" I asked.

"I think I will call him Gunny," Emmi said, laughing at his antics. "Hopefully, someone will be missing him and call us."

After she was done with the intake, had vaccinated him, and once again checked for a microchip, she walked Gunny back to the dog runs to put him inside a kennel. Even though she left him with a nice bed, food, and lots of toys, he howled unhappily.

We learned in the coming weeks that Gunny needed to be with people. He became very woebegone and unhappy when left alone in his kennel. When the ten-day hold was up, we scheduled him to be neutered and micro-chipped so we could start the adoption process.

I did his evaluation and reposted him on our website as available. After a week with no one showing any interest, I looked at the pictures that had been taken of him. He looked menacing in them, so we took another round of pictures, positioning him with toys, people, and children.

We were perplexed when we looked at the new pictures because no matter how many we took, he still looked intimidating. We could not seem to capture Gunny's true, endearing personality. So we posted the pictures back up on the website and hoped for the best.

One day, when some gang members walked through dressed in their distinctive clothes, colors, and tattoos, wanting to visit with Gunny, we knew we were in trouble.

I wrote a long article about him, but potential adopters still showed no interest. The longer he stayed with us, the more stressed he became. Soon he was barking, chewing up his bed, destroying his toys, and jumping on the front of his kennel. People quickly walked by and would not stop to interact with him.

I knew why they were not interested in him, and I understood. They must have thought this huge eight-month-old puppy, who weighed around ninety pounds, would completely demolish their homes.

If a potential adopter showed interest and wanted to take him outdoors to get acquainted, Gunny, in all his exuberance and excitement, would lunge forward, dragging them behind him as he ran toward the play yard.

None of the staff was willing to take him home, and every day he remained with us he became more stressed.

We called several trainers, hoping someone would help train him to become a good canine citizen. A trainer came forward, and we happily waved goodbye to Gunny. He would be with her for a month-long training course at her home.

Not only would he get training, but a professional would also see him in a home setting.

A month later, when the trainer returned with Gunny, his manners were impeccable. He sat, lay down, and heeled beautifully with no thought of pulling or jumping on someone.

"He is a big, strong teenage puppy with a very gentle heart," the trainer said. "He loves everyone and never meets a stranger."

Emmi reached down to pet Gunny, impressed with his new manners.

"Now, because he has learned excellent skills," she said, "maybe someone will be interested in adopting him."

The trainer handed Gunny's training certificate to Emmi.

"Put this certificate with his paperwork," she said. "It should help him get adopted, and it shows he has completed the training course."

We all loved Gunny's new skills and knew they would impress a potential adopter. I immediately rewrote his biography, posted it on the website, and then we waited for a response.

It worked, and before the week was over, Gunny went home with his new owner. She was a single lady who lived by herself at the end of a country lane. I had been away for a couple of days and heard the news upon my return.

"What is she like?" I asked Heather.

"A little strange, but very nice," was her answer.

"What do you mean, strange?" I inquired.

"Oh, I do not know. It is hard to put into words."

"Eccentric, odd, weird," Pat said cynically, without looking up.

Now my curiosity was piqued, mixed with a little apprehension, and I was feeling nervous for Gunny.

"Come on, you two, you are making me very uneasy about this adoption," I said.

"Oh, she is okay," Heather retorted. "Gunny will have good care, and he has a couple of acres to run in."

"She gave me the heebie-jeebies," Pat said.

The conversation stalled, and I could not get any more information from them.

As the weeks went by, we did not hear from Gunny's new owner, so we presumed all was going well.

Then about three months later, she walked through the doors with Gunny.

When I saw her, I knew what Pat meant by eccentric and weird.

Her long, graying hair was uncombed and frizzed, sticking out from beneath her knitted cap. It looked as if she had been shocked by a jolt of electricity. Her clothes had stains of old paint and had faded from many washings. Her denim shirt was missing buttons and held together with safety pins.

Her sleeves were rolled up, exposing her lower arms, and her hands were crippled and curled with arthritis.

But it was her face that was the most revealing. I could see that at one time she had been beautiful, but as time aged her, she had taken on a witchy look. When she looked at me, she had the most penetrating gray-gold eyes I had ever seen. They seemed mythical as she looked directly at you, causing me to look away.

I expected her voice to crackle with harshness, but, it had almost a musical sound, like a soft flowing brook.

"Hi, my name is Penelope," she said, sticking out her weathered hand to shake mine.

"I have come to return the dog."

"You mean Gunny?" I asked her, shaking her crippled hand.

"Yes, Gunny, the dog."

"Can I ask what the problem is?" I questioned.

"The brute hates my bird," she stated, furrowing her eyebrows. "My crow and the dog, they hate each other and fight all the time. One of them has to go, and it will not be my bird," she declared in her soft voice.

"Is that the only problem you have had with him?"

"Yes, that is the only problem, but one or the other is going to get hurt, and I will not have it."

Her voice became even softer, and I tried to listen while avoiding her steady stare.

"Last night they got into another fight, and I was worried that Gem was going to peck the dog's eye out."

Now her voice had become a whisper, and I did not want to lean any closer to hear it.

I turned to pick up a release form, which Pat already had in her hand, holding it out toward me. I could read Pat's facial expression of mistrust of this woman, and also relief that Gunny was being returned.

Penelope spent the next few minutes filling out the papers as she quietly muttered to herself. When she was done, she handed them back to me.

I took the papers from her crippled hand and thanked her for bringing Gunny back.

"What did you name him?" I asked.

"Dog," she said in a low voice, looking at me quizzically. "He is just a dog."

She walked out to her old 1950 Chevy truck, which at one time had been green but was now mostly rust, and drove away.

Gunny and I stood watching her as Pat walked up beside us.

"I told you she was weird."

She threw up her hands, annoyed.

"Jeez! She did not even name him," she said, exasperated.

"Dog," she exclaimed. "She did not call her bird crow."

Turning, she left to go back to work, but I stood there mesmerized by the encounter, as if bewitched.

We put Gunny back into a kennel, glad that he was back, and started the adoption process all over again.

Two weeks after his return, a young man walked into the shelter.

He was wearing a camouflage vest with all kinds of badges, ribbons, medallions, and decorations that signify the United States Marine Corps. He was muscular, stood tall and straight as he waited courteously on the other side of the front counter for someone to acknowledge him.

"How can I help you?" Heather asked.

"Yes, Ma'am, thank you, Ma'am, for asking," he answered politely. "My name is Ben, and I am here to see Gunny."

"Do you have an appointment to see Gunny?"

"No, Ma'am, I did not realize I would need one," he replied.

"Well, you do not," Heather said, laughing. "I just like being called Ma'am."

He looked at her good-naturedly, still holding a respectful Marine stance.

Heather told him about Gunny and then questioned Ben about himself.

"I have received my discharge papers from the Marines and was told a dog may help with my PTSD. I could wait for a dog from the training program," he said. "But since I have trained dogs, they said they would come alongside me to help train the dog I choose."

He still stood straight, but a smile touched his mouth.

"I was reading on your website about Gunny, and I think he may work for me."

Heather went to the drawer to get an application form. After she handed it to him, she texted me asking if I would come to the front desk. When I got there, Heather introduced Ben to me.

"This is Ben," Heather said. "And he is interested in Gunny. He wants him for a service dog."

"Hi, Ben," I said, holding out my hand. "So you are interested in Gunny?"

"Yes, Ma'am," he said, shaking my hand. "I have signed up for the Battle Buddies training program."

"What do you know about the Mastiff breed?" I asked him.

"I have read extensively on them and know they are guardian dogs," he answered. "I read they are generally easygoing, patient, stoic, calm, and loyal. Your website said he is a young dog and has been with a trainer."

I invited him into the office, and we sat down together to visit while he filled out the application. I was impressed that he knew so much about training dogs and how much he had investigated Gunny's breed.

"Did you know Mastiffs will check on their owner five to seven times a night?" he asked, looking at me closely.

"I have heard that," I answered.

"I have flashbacks and nightmares, and I need a dog who will wake me," he said.

"I have heard of the Battle Buddies program," I said. "But I have never met anyone who has been through it. It sounds like a great program for veterans."

"Yes, Ma'am, I have a great support group of men and women who have been through the program and received their dogs. It is a demanding training program with great results for both dogs and their handlers. After I have completed the training, I will be able to come alongside other veterans who suffer with PTSD."

He looked at me intently.

"What do you think? Do you think Gunny would work out in service?"

"Gunny is very intuitive and sensitive," I told him. "He wants to be with people all the time, so I think he could work very well for you."

While he completed the application, I went across the hall to talk with our director. As I reached her door, Heather handed me information on the Northwest Battle Buddies Foundation.

With the information in hand, we knocked on the director's door and went in.

"We have a young man in the office across the hall who is interested in Gunny," Heather stated. "He is a veteran who served in the Marines and now suffers from PTSD."

Our director sat back in her chair, ready to listen.

"He would like Gunny as a service dog and has enrolled in

a training program for service dogs called Battle Buddies," I told her.

I slid the information across the desk toward her. Our director picked up the pamphlet on the organization to read while I continued to talk.

"He has trained dogs before, so they have accepted him into the program early."

She set the information down on her desktop, looking intently toward us.

"So now," she said, "he needs a dog, and you both think it could be Gunny?"

We both nodded in agreement.

"The Mastiff breed are guardian dogs," I said to her. "They will check on their owners several times a night. We all know how much Gunny loves people and wants to be with them all the time. So yes, I think Gunny could work well for him."

Whenever our director was deep in thought and considering something, she always tapped her pen on her desktop. Pulling her glasses down, she looked at both of us.

"Well," she said, tapping her pen a couple more times, "why don't you bring this young man into my office so I can meet him?"

Heather went across the hall to get Ben and brought him into her office to meet her. Introducing them, she shut the door behind her so they could visit.

Heather and I stayed close to the front desk. We were excited for Gunny and knew this would be a good placement for him.

When our director's door opened, she waved me over.

"Would you go get Gunny so Ben can meet him?"

I ran down the hall, grabbing a harness and leash. As I approached Gunny's kennel, I stopped and quietly stood still trying to calm myself. When I went inside with him, Gunny remained relaxed. I whispered as I harnessed him and clipped the leash on. Then putting my head on his, I tried to communicate to him how special he would be for this young man. We walked together down the hall towards my director's office. When I opened her door, Ben was no longer sitting there.

"What happened?" I asked, worried that Ben had changed his mind.

"He's across the hall with Heather," she said, smiling. "They are ready to do the adoption if Ben thinks Gunny will work out for him."

I turned Gunny around to head into the other office. Opening the door, Gunny walked in ahead of me, and Ben stood up. Gunny's training paid off as he calmly greeted Ben with good manners.

In a low voice, Ben acknowledged Gunny, calling him over so he could pet him. Heather and I left the office so they could become acquainted. We stood behind the front counter and watched them through the office window.

Once Ben felt that Gunny was comfortable with him, he leaned down to handle Gunny's feet, look in his mouth, and quietly play with him. If Gunny walked away, Ben would recall him back over to him.

When we came back into the office, Ben asked if he could take Gunny outdoors for a walk. As I watched them walk down the sidewalk together, I could tell they were bonding.

When they returned, Ben looked in our direction with a smile, and I knew Gunny had won his heart.

"I would like to give this a try," he said. "What do you think, Gunny? Would you like to go into service and come home with a Marine?"

We adopted Gunny to Ben that afternoon, and as we always do, we stood at the door to wave them off and hope for a good outcome for both the dog and his person.

Ben kept us informed on Gunny's progress while they were in the training program. He told us Gunny excelled with all his training and what a great dog he had become for him.

Watching over Ben at night, Gunny would wake him when he was having one of his horrific nightmares. Ben told us he was more confident and relaxed with Gunny at his side.

After completing the program, he became a trainer in the Northwest Battle Buddies Program.

We were so happy with the outcome for both of them, and it was gratifying to know that one of our dogs had become a service dog for one of our American heroes.

Happy for Ben, who had received the help and support he needed, and he was now helping others who were entering the program. And happy for Gunny, who was making a difference by serving and helping a veteran regain his freedom and independence.

Ben brought Gunny over to see us one afternoon. He came through the front door next to his handler, wearing a camouflage service vest with a Marine emblem on it and his NWBB badge.

"He has been a great dog for me," Ben said, smiling.

"And you kept his name?" I asked.

"Yes, Ma'am. He is a Marine," he answered.

As I watched them drive away, it was another proud moment for me and all our team at the Humane Society.

To think! A dog who was abandoned in a park served a Marine who needed his help.

Oorah!

Never Quit, Never Give Up

It is our hope that the day before a

Veteran meets their service dog is
their last worst day...
and the day they meet their service dog it is
their best first day.

SHARON WALKER, CEO & FOUNDER
NWBB

LAURA

If there is ever going to be a fight among the public at the shelter, it will be when a West Highland Terrier, Golden Retriever, or Yorkshire Terrier comes into the Humane Society to be placed for adoption. Our phones will start ringing endlessly, and people will flood into the shelter to place an application for them.

After filling out the application, some will think they are first in line to get the dog, but we also take applications through the mail and on our website. We keep the application process open for a short time and then close it. Once we have enough, we sort through them, reading each one.

We will place the applications in different categories so we can match the dogs to the homes that are best suited for them.

Many things come into consideration before we make our decision. Does the person rent or own? Some landlords do not allow dogs, some exclude certain breeds, and some have weight restrictions.

Does the applicant live close to a busy road? If so, do they have a fenced yard? Do they have a plan to keep the dog safe?

Are there children or grandchildren living in or visiting the home? Some dogs do not care for children, while other dogs love them.

Do they have other animals in their home? We do meet-and-greets with the applicant's dog to see if their dog likes the new dog who would be coming to live with them.

Does the applicant own a cat or livestock? Some dogs do not care for cats or may not be good around livestock.

Does the applicant understand the energy levels of certain breeds? Will they be able to give the dog the stimulation it will need to be happy?

Can they afford veterinary bills? Some dogs come to the Humane Society with health issues and will need veterinary care.

Once the applications are read and considered, we then choose a home.

If the dog belongs to one of the breeds I mentioned above— West Highland Terrier, Golden Retriever, Yorkshire Terrier, and a few others—people may get very upset if they are not selected.

A few people become indignant, feeling they have been overlooked. Some will bully us over the phone or at the front desk. Some will write a nasty message on our website or go on social media to tell the world how inept, incompetent, and mean-spirited we are.

Some have resorted to name-calling and displayed the worst kind of human behavior while demanding the dog. And then the final group is the people who bribe us with money and try to buy the dog.

The problem is we have one dog and many applications, and it is impossible to make everyone happy.

What is refreshing is the many wonderful people who, after putting in an application, quietly and respectfully wait. How does the saying go? Patience is a virtue. Because of their kindness and understanding, their application is usually prioritized at the top of the pile.

Laura, a beautiful Golden Retriever, came into the shelter one day, causing this kind of commotion. Applications piled in, and our phones started ringing as soon as we placed her on the website.

Her owner had died, leaving her in the care of an only daughter who owned a cat.

While she filled out the personality profile on her deceased mother's dog, she told us, "Laura hates cats! That is why I am not keeping her."

Emmi looked across the desk at the Golden Retriever next to this serene-acting woman, surprised.

"You must mean she is playing and chases them for fun," she questioned.

"No!" the woman replied adamantly. "I mean, she hates them."

Emmi looked back and forth between the dog and the woman, unsure, because it is so out of character for a Golden Retriever to hate anything.

The woman continued to fill out the paperwork, and after she finished, she handed the dog over to Emmi and left.

Emmi called my office and informed me that someone had surrendered a Golden Retriever. I went to meet Laura and sat down to read her paperwork.

"The lady who surrendered her says she hates cats," Emmi informed me.

"What!" I said, surprised.

Laura had walked over to me and was leaning against my leg. She placed her head in my lap and looked up at me with gentle eyes.

"Do you really hate cats?" I asked, laughing.

She was a beautiful three-year-old dog with long golden hair that flowed and shimmered in the light. Looking at me, her forehead furrowed with worry.

Reaching toward her, I stroked her down her back, talking quietly.

Looking across the room, I noticed people standing outside the office window, smiling and pointing.

"Well, girl," I said, holding her head in my hands, "it looks like you are a celebrity already."

Emmi picked up the microchip scanner and moved it down Laura's neck and between her shoulder blades. Beep, beep, beep sounded the scanner, with the numbers showing on the screen. She quickly jotted down and got up to leave.

"I will call the microchip company to make sure she is registered to the right person."

She was gone for about twenty minutes before returning.

"Not the same owner," she informed me, frowning. "She is registered to someone in Seattle."

"Uh-oh," I replied.

I looked toward all the smiling people crowding around the office window, and Emmi followed my gaze.

"I will tell them she is micro-chipped to someone else, and we have to follow protocol before taking applications on her," she said.

She walked out of the office to explain to everyone that Laura was micro-chipped and we would not be taking applications until we contacted the owner. I could tell from their reactions that they were disappointed. Picking up a leash, I snapped it tono Laura's collar so we could wade through the adoring crowd. Laura, calm and even-tempered, wagged her tail congenially as she walked past each person.

When we arrived in the North Wing, I found a cozy kennel where she would be out of the public eye. Once the person she was registered to was notified, we would know why someone else had taken ownership of her. Meanwhile, the word was out, the shelter phones were ringing, and applications were pouring in like an upstream dam that had overflowed.

Emmi spent the next three days trying to contact the person on Laura's microchip. He finally returned her call and confirmed he had been the original owner. He told Emmi he had gotten Laura as a puppy, and when he separated from his girlfriend, he left Laura with her. He confirmed the deceased woman was Laura's owner, and she must have failed to change the microchip to her name. He was not interested in keeping Laura and agreed to put her up for adoption. His only request was that she be placed in a nice home. With the microchip mystery cleared up, I could do her evaluation, and then we would begin the adoption process.

"The daughter claimed she hates cats," I informed everyone at the front desk.

"Oh, for heaven's sake," Pat exclaimed. "She is a Golden Retriever; they love everyone."

"Not according to the daughter," I stated. "It says on her intake profile she hates cats. That is why she could not keep her."

"Oh, that was just an excuse," Pat said, brushing me off. "She just did not want her."

"Well, I guess I will find out during her evaluation," I said.

Pat picked up the stack of applications, waving them in front of me.

"Look at these. If you are right, we will meticulously have to go through each one and pick out the ones who own a cat."

"Yes, you will," I retorted.

"What is going on?" our director said, popping out of her office.

Pat stood there with her hands on her hips, looking at the stack of applications.

"Laura is not only starting brawls with the public; she is starting quarrels with staff," Emmi laughed.

"Let Julie do the evaluation," our director said firmly.

Looking down at the large stack of applications, she shook her head.

"After Laura's evaluation, we will all sit down and start going through this mountain."

She walked back into her office, closing the door behind her. Pat tossed her head indignantly as I grabbed Laura's paperwork out of the intake book and left.

Laura's kennel was empty when I went back to get her, but hanging on the front of her kennel was a placard saying: "I am out for a walk." A volunteer must have taken her to the play yard, so I hurried outdoors to retrieve her.

They were sitting on a bench in the warm sun, and the volunteer was combing Laura's luxurious coat. Sarah had been a devoted and loyal member of our volunteer team for several years. Quietly, she came and went each week to walk dogs. Most of the time, she took out senior dogs who were harder to adopt because of their age. Even though Laura was not an old dog, Sarah added her to her list.

When I approached them, she looked at me guiltily and smiled.

"I know she is receiving a lot of attention from everyone, but I love the Golden Retriever breed."

"She is beautiful," I replied.

"I had a Golden when I was a little girl," she said. "They love to be doted on."

"I can tell she is enjoying being here with you," I laughed.

Laura lifted a front paw to touch Sarah's leg, reminding her to keep brushing.

"I know," Sarah murmured to Laura. "You love being combed, don't you? Placing both hands over Laura's ears, she gently kissed the top of her head.

"Laura reminds me of my first dog when I was a child," she told me, with a far-off look in her eyes.

"My mum brought home a Golden Retriever puppy named Sadie after my dad died in a car accident. She probably knew I would be sad and lonely, and thought a puppy would help me with my grief.

"And did it?" I asked, looking at her intently.

"Oh yes. Sadie made me laugh again, and just having her close to me was nice."

Pausing in memory, she soon continued. "After my dad's death, Mum went to work, and when I came home from school, the house seemed empty and cold. But after I got Sadie, it seemed less lonely."

She looked at me closely to see if I understood.

"Dogs are great therapists," I told her. "They bring a lot of comfort when we are hurting."

I knew Sarah had gone through more tragedy in her life this last year, after her husband had died from cancer. She had recently returned after being away for a while and was now spending more time walking dogs.

"Do you have a dog now?" I asked.

"No, I rent, and I am not sure I can have a dog."

"Well, at least check with your landlord," I told her. "A dog would have an excellent home with you."

"Maybe I should," she said, smiling.

"Would you mind if I take Laura from you?" I asked. "I need to do her evaluation."

"No, I do not mind," she said, handing the leash to me.

"You be a good girl," she told Laura, waving goodbye.

I picked up Laura's leash and took her inside to evaluate

her. In my office, she smelled around the room and then lay down beside me with a toy. Goldens have such an affectionate personality, and Laura personified the breed with her calm and quiet nature.

She lay on the rug content and happy, wagging her tail each time I looked at her. She stood up and moved close to show me her toy, then gently laid her head on my lap so she could look up at me with her tranquil eyes.

If ever a dog can captivate and win your heart, it is the Golden Retriever. Once she received the desired pats and attention, she politely picked up her toy and walked over to her bed to lie down. Sighing, she laid her head down on her front feet, using the toy as a pillow.

Her evaluation went well, and I knew the ultimate test would be with cats. I called her over and clipped her leash onto her collar.

Once outdoors, we walked toward the barn, where the chickens were contentedly pecking in the grass. Laura happily pranced beside me, enjoying the fresh air, acting as if she did not have a care in the world.

When she noticed the chickens, she stopped to watch them and then looked back at me as if to say:

"Are you coming?"

I was relieved when she ignored them and continued with our stroll. Because it was such a nice day, I was caught up in the warm, sunny moments we were sharing. I think she had lulled me into her Golden Retriever charm, and I should have known better than to relax.

It was her low growl that startled me back to reality. Before I could brace myself, she jerked on the leash with all her strength, yanking it out of my hand.

Moving with remarkable speed, she sprinted toward a feral

cat who was running for her life. I yelled at Laura to stop, but she was fixated with no intention of halting.

Even when the cat had safely scooted under the fence and disappeared inside the barn, Laura continued to run back and forth along the fence, ferociously barking. The scruff on her neck and back was high, and she was ready for battle, determined to get to the cat. She was digging under the fence when I ran up behind her and grabbed her leash.

"Bad girl," I scolded as I tried to pull her away.

Her obsession had consumed her, and she had no intention of leaving her prey behind. Pulling her away from the fence, I tried to walk her away. She resisted and did not want to leave, so I had to drag her back toward the shelter. She finally submitted, but she did not forget the cat and continued to look back toward the barn.

I knew I would not be testing Laura with our shelter cat, who helped me with evaluations. She had been my partner for years, but I would never knowingly put her in danger, and it was evident Laura did not like cats.

Because of her dislike for cats, I knew she could not go into a home with them, so when we walked through the shelter doors, I told the staff:

"No cats," I said. "She hates them."

Emmi shook her head in agreement.

"Okay, we are pulling the applications of people who own cats."

I took Laura back to my office and pulled her profile up on the website and typed:

"No cats under any circumstances."

I clicked save and sent it over to my director.

When we came back indoors on the day of Laura's evaluation, I noticed a woman standing at the front desk. She introduced herself to Emmi and told her she had come to visit with Laura and put an application on her.

"I am sorry," Emmi said. "We have closed the applications for Laura and are not taking any more."

"I drove all the way from Edmonds, so I am sure one more application will not make a lot of difference," Beth told Emmi.

"We have other dogs who are looking for a home. Would you be interested in looking at one of them?" Emmi responded.

"I have adopted from you before and have always owned Goldens," Beth insisted.

Emmi could tell she was going to have a problem, and frankly, she was weary of the whole situation. Because Beth had adopted from us before, Emmi decided to give her an application to fill out, but before she handed it to her, she had a question.

"Do you own a cat?"

Beth shook her head adamantly.

"I assure you, I do not," she said firmly. "I do not care for cats."

So Emmi relented and handed Beth an application. When Beth had filled it out, Emmi put it with the other thirty applications in the file. Now there were thirty-one.

After Beth drove away, Emmi turned to the staff and informed them not to take any more applications on Laura.

Two days later, Emmi, our director, and two other staff members sat down to go through the applications on Laura. They removed any applications from the pile if the applicants had cats, leaving ten applications. Sorting through the ten, four applications stood out, and everyone felt they would be great homes for Laura. Two of them were Sarah, the volunteer, and Beth's.

Talking back and forth, they narrowed it down to Sarah and Beth. I walked into the meeting as they were looking at the two finalists. When I found out Sarah was one of them, I campaigned for her.

"She is here three times a week," I told them. "And Laura already knows her."

"I know, but I really like this application," our director said, holding Beth's in her hand. "Beth has adopted from us before, and I am concerned because Sarah rents."

Emmi picked up Sarah's application to read it again.

"Sarah's son is her landlord, and he told me she could have a dog," she said.

Looking closely at both applications, our director laid one down in front of Emmi.

"I think we should go with Beth," she said, with her mind made up.

Since the decision had been made, Emmi left the room to call Beth and arrange for her to finalize the adoption.

Beth was ecstatic and came to the shelter the next day to complete the adoption and take Laura home. We called Sarah to tell her another home had been chosen for Laura.

The following day, when Sarah came in to walk dogs, I could tell she was disappointed, but because of her unselfish nature, she reassured us of her happiness for Laura.

"I know it was a tough decision for all of you. I just feel bad I did not get to say goodbye to her," she said sadly.

"Would you be interested in taking one of the other dogs?" Emmi asked.

"Of course, but I want to take my time," she said, smiling. "I will know the right one when I meet her."

Sarah was such an understanding person, and I felt bad she was not picked for Laura. Later in the afternoon, I saw her sitting in the play yard with another dog, combing his coat and doting on him.

It was early the next morning, before we opened, when

Emmi noticed Beth outside the shelter doors with Laura. She went and opened the door for Beth. Agitated, Beth ran toward her and threw Laura's leash toward her.

"I cannot keep her," she said as she nervously paced.

"Come in so you can tell me what happened," Emmi told her.

Beth came in, and Emmi escorted her to her office. Emmi sat down to talk with her while Beth paced back and forth, flailing her arms. Watching through the office window, I could not imagine what had gone wrong.

"What happened?" Emmi asked.

"I have done an awful thing," Beth answered, tears in her eyes. "I am so selfish."

"Sit down," Emmi said, pointing to a chair.

Beth would not sit but continued to pace back and forth while she made her confession to Emmi.

"I did not believe your evaluator," she said, wringing her hands. "I overheard her say Laura was not good with cats, and when you asked me if I owned cats, I told you I did not. I lied to you."

After her confession, she sat down and put her hands over her face. Emmi waved for Heather and me to come into the office.

When we heard what Beth had done, we looked at each other, surprised. I was immediately worried that Laura had hurt Beth's cat.

"Did Laura harm your cat?" Emmi asked.

"No," Beth said, shaking her head behind her hands. Then, looking up, she told us what had happened.

"All went well after I got Laura home. We played ball together and then went for a walk around the neighborhood. When I got her inside the house, I fed her and took her to the living room so we could snuggle together on the sofa.

I was watching TV, and Laura had her head in my lap, relaxed. I thought she had fallen asleep, and my cat walked into the living room. Laura saw her and flew off the couch, barking and growling. Gabby was running for her life, and Laura was close behind, snapping at her with her teeth.

She chased her into the bedroom and under the bed. Laura started digging and tearing up the carpet, determined to get to her. She acted as if she had lost her mind.

I grabbed her by the collar and dragged her out of the bedroom and shut the door.

When I released her, she started digging at the carpet and scratched up the bedroom door. She was determined to get back inside, and I could not get her to stop.

Finally, I pulled her into the laundry room, shutting her in there. She acted crazy and was digging at the door to get out. I was afraid if I let her out, she would go back to hunt for my cat.

I got some blankets and slept on the laundry room floor with her. This morning, when I let her out to feed her, she ran straight to my bedroom door and started barking and digging at the carpet again."

We listened to Beth's harrowing experience of the night before and tried to be sympathetic to what she had endured. When I looked at Emmi and Heather, I could see their lips twitching in suppressed smiles.

I was not smiling. This event happened because Beth foolishly did not believe what I had discovered in Laura's evaluation, and I did not find it amusing.

"Did you not stop to think there a reason I said no cats?" I asked, frustrated by the situation.

Beth sat straight up, defensive.

"I have owned dogs for years, and I have never had anything like this happen before," she said.

Raising her hands in the air, she spread them in front of her.

"I thought I could handle it," she said, frustrated. "After all, she is a Golden Retriever."

"A Golden Retriever who hates cats," I replied.

Her shoulders sank before she answered me.

"I guess I thought you were exaggerating, and I wanted her."

Heather pulled the return-to-shelter form out of the desk so Beth could fill it out. I took Laura and put her inside my office. I was so irritated with Beth because she had put Laura in such a compromising situation. Laura could have harmed her cat or, worse yet, bitten Beth. It was all out of selfishness and her personal need, because she wanted a certain breed of dog.

After Beth left, I went back into the office to talk with Heather and Emmi about the mornings events.

"How did she know to lie?" I asked.

"She heard you say no cats," Emmi said. "I specifically asked her if she had cats in her home, and she denied owning one."

"Well, a lesson learned," Heather said. "Serves her right."

Later in the morning, when our director arrived, we gathered inside her office to inform her of the morning events. Listening to what had happened, she tapped her pen irritably on her desktop.

"Well," she said, throwing the pen down. "Some people have to learn the hard way."

I knew she was exasperated, but then she started laughing. Not just a chuckle, but a hilarious, uproarious, side-splitting laugh. She laughed until tears rolled down her cheeks, and between hoots she choked out the words:

"You are telling me she had to sleep on the floor of the laundry room?"

She laughed harder.

Now I could see the comedy of the entire event. Remembering Beth with her hair disheveled and the frantic look on her face, I started laughing with the others.

"Serves her right," our director announced, still guffawing.

"Call Sarah," she tittered. "And see if she still wants to adopt Laura."

We left her office to call Sarah, and after we closed her door, we heard another outburst of laughter.

Sarah did want Laura, and because we did not want another cat incident, we asked her if she owned a cat. She assured us she did not, so the next day Sarah came to adopt Laura.

We waved goodbye after completing the adoption, knowing it was a permanent placement in a cat-free zone.

Through the years, more Golden Retrievers, Yorkies, and sought-after dogs would come into the Humane Society. Once again, we would go through the same undesirable behavior people display who love the breeds.

It is wonderful when people love and desire these breeds, but please do not forget there are thirty or more dogs in the shelter who are waiting for a home. They also need your love and affection just as much. Because they are not a sought-after breed, their stay at the shelter may be much longer before being placed in a home. They too would make great dogs and companions for you if you give them a chance.

Laura was just an example of how people will lose their minds, and it could have been a disaster. She could have hurt the cat or harmed the person who was attempting to stop her.

When it comes to adoptions, we are not complacent, and we work very hard to place every dog in a suitable home. We do not want a bad outcome for the dog or the people who adopt them.

Sarah ended up adopting Laura, and it was a wonderful placement for both of them.

Sarah would occasionally bring Laura to the shelter to visit us. Before coming, she would call so we could put our shelter cat in her kennel. Laura, in her Golden Retriever's great nature, serenely greeted all of us, sprinkling out her devotion to make each person feel special.

When they were leaving, Sarah would look down at Laura and smile.

"She has been a great dog, and I love her," she said. "But she still hates cats."

Laura is a constant reminder for us to remain diligent when looking for a home for each animal in our care. We often think of the quote from Beth:

"After all, she is just a Golden Retriever."

Golden Retriever or not, she still hated cats.

Dogs never lie about love.

JEFFERY MOUSSAIEFF MASSON

HOUSTON

"Houston, we have a problem." That was going to be our new mantra as we repeated it to each other for the next four months.

Houston came to us as a transfer from a shelter in another state. Before he arrived, he was treated for a wound at the back of his right shoulder, close to the rib cage. He was seen by their shelter veterinarian and treated for an abscess they thought was caused by a dog fight. He had been with them for several weeks, and after treatment the wound had closed and looked healed. So the veterinarian signed his health certificate authorizing the transfer.

They flew him to our shelter in the valley in early June with another group of dogs. On arrival, we looked inside his carrier to see a beautiful Miniature Schnauzer. He was silver-grey in color, with a short undercoat and a hard, wiry outer coat. He had a comical face with dark brown eyes and bushy eyebrows. At the end of his long muzzle was a black button nose, and under his chin he sported a long, dense, bushy beard. Standing straight on his front legs, his back legs leaned back,

49

pushing his back into a straight line. His stub tail pointed up, and he wagged it stiffly back and forth in friendliness. He was a dapper fellow, exuberant and lively, showing off a comical character, and we were amused by him.

"Yap, yap, yap," he barked. "Yap, yap."

Barking is common to the Schnauzer breed, and he was making sure his voice was heard. Schnauzers are alert, intelligent, spirited, and they like people. We were excited to have him at our shelter and knew he would quickly find a home.

"What is his name?" someone asked.

I turned his placard over to read it.

"Houston," I said.

Everyone laughed out loud, thinking it appropriate, because he had arrived from Texas.

The volunteers were enthralled and had fallen in love with Houston. A volunteer named Ken was very fond of him and visited the shelter daily. Houston romped and showed off, enjoying his playtime with Ken.

"Yap, yap, yap," we would hear, followed by Ken's laughter.

Ken had come from Georgia and was working at the refinery on a turnaround for the next three months. He did not have any family or friends here and did not like being cooped up in a motel room with nothing to do. He thought his time would go by faster if he could volunteer somewhere, so he chose the Humane Society. He told us he wanted to connect with the local community and help out.

Even though Ken would be with the shelter for a short time, we were excited to have him, because every person who volunteers makes a difference in an animal's life. Ken went through the volunteer orientation and training so he could walk dogs. Because he worked the evening shift at the refinery, he came to the shelter in the afternoon after waking up.

Not long after he started walking dogs, he discovered Houston. With his happy, carefree personality, Houston wiggled his way into Ken's heart. Playing together in the play yard, we could hear Ken laughing at Houston's clownish behaviors. After spending time outdoors, Ken would often bring Houston into my office for a visit.

"He learned to sit today," Ken said proudly one afternoon.

Looking down at Houston, he gave the command to sit. Instead, Houston brushed off the command and jumped onto Ken's lap, licking him on the face. Admiring Houston and forgiving him for not sitting, he looked at me with a sheepish grin.

"He really does sit," Ken said, as if trying to convince me. "He is just a bit of a rebel."

"I believe you," I said, not wanting to discourage him from his hard work and also understanding how stubborn the Schnauzer breed is.

"Have you started taking applications on him yet?" Ken inquired.

"Not yet," I replied. "Which reminds me, I need to check his wound area to make sure it is still healed."

Even though the veterinarian had given him a clean bill of health, we were checking Houston every day to make sure the wound had not come back. I patted my lap, and Houston jumped from Ken's to mine. Because he was so wiggly, Ken held him in place so I could check his injury.

"It is looking good," I said, smiling.

Carefully, I felt around the wound.

"I think by next week, we will be able to post him on the website."

Ken ruffled his coat.

"Did you hear that, Houston? Next week everyone will be able to look at your handsome face."

The following week I prepared Houston's write-up and

was ready to post him on our website. His evaluation had gone well, and I felt confident that he had fully recovered from his injury. I had just typed his evaluation into the computer when there was a knock on my door. Ken stepped in, holding Houston, with a concerned look.

"Would you check Houston's shoulder?" he asked, sitting Houston down on my lap.

I looked at the wound area. It was red and swollen, with a small amount of discharge. He winced in pain when I felt around it.

I texted Emmi.

"Houston, we have a problem," I said. "Would you come into my office?" When she came in, I showed her Houston's old injury.

"Wow, that is not good," she said. "It looked fine yesterday. I will call Dr. Vincent to see if he can see him as soon as possible."

"Oh, oh," I interjected. "Remember, Dr. Vincent will be out of town for the next three weeks."

"Oh, that is right!" Emmi responded, disappointed. "I will have to call around to see if we can get him into another vet clinic."

She reached out to touch Ken on his arm.

"If I can get a vet to see Houston today, would you be willing to drive him there?"

"Sure, anything for my little friend," he said, concerned.

Emmi left to make some calls. She returned in about twenty minutes and told us she had found a veterinarian who would see him in an hour.

"I have faxed his medical history over to the clinic so they will know what kind of treatment he received before he was transferred to us."

We got a carrier for Houston and helped Ken load him into

his car. They were gone for a couple of hours before returning. Ken handed Emmi a sack filled with medicine and instructions on wound care.

"The veterinarian told me some infections are very hard to clear up," Ken said. "But she is optimistic that another round of antibiotics with this topical cream will take care of it."

We emptied the contents of the sack onto the countertop. It contained an antibiotic and topical cream with instructions on how to carefully clean and treat Houston's wound.

We started his treatment immediately. Because the wound had recurred, we had to place Houston on a fourteen-day medical hold, and we would not be able to post him on the website until he had a clean bill of health.

We examined the wound daily for the next two weeks. After a couple of days, the wound started to close and again turned a healthy pink. We were relieved and confident the new medicine had worked and Houston was on the mend.

Ken kept a watchful eye on him when taking him out each day to play. Like a proud parent, he bragged to the staff about Houston's many achievements. He had taught him to sit, lie down, sit up, and to speak, but to Ken's chagrin, Houston stubbornly refused to perform the tricks he had supposedly learned.

Another two weeks went by, and the wound looked healed. We moved him into East Wing to start his adoption process.

Four days later, Ken came into my office with a distressed look on his face, holding Houston in his arms. He turned him around to show me his shoulder, and I could see the wound was looking inflamed again. I immediately called Emmi back to my office, and when she opened my door, I pointed over at Houston.

"Houston, we have a problem," I said, frustrated.

She rushed over to look at Houston's shoulder. Her brown eyes looked at me, wide with disbelief.

"I cannot believe it," she said, stunned. "I just looked at it yesterday, and it looked great. What the heck!"

"I know," I said, shaking my head. "I also saw him yesterday, and it looked fine."

She picked him up, taking him to the director's office with Ken and me following close behind her.

"What is up?" our director asked as we crammed into her office.

Emmi set Houston down on her lap so she could look at his back.

"I thought he was on antibiotics?" She said, questioning us.

"He was," Emmi stated. "He just finished them, and yesterday his wound looked great, but today we found it inflamed again."

"Poor little guy," our director said, gently petting him. "We'd better get him to Dr. Vincent."

"He is still out of town," Emmi told her.

"Well, let me call to see if we can get him back to the last veterinarian who treated him," our director said, picking up her phone to call. We went back to my office. Ken put Houston down on the floor, and he ran to the toy box to pick out a squeaky toy to play with.

Ten minutes later, our director came to my office to tell us that the veterinarian who had seen him was out of town at a conference.

"I have called another vet clinic," she informed us, "and they will see him tomorrow."

The next day, Emmi loaded up Houston to take him to another veterinarian. She returned with a different antibiotic and more instructions on how to treat his wound.

"The vet told me dog bites can be very hard to clear up," she told us.

When Ken came by later in the afternoon, I could tell he was hesitant and still worried about Houston.

We spent another ten days cleaning Houston's wound and medicating him with more medicine. The new veterinarian had given Houston a stronger antibiotic and a different topical cream. Now, at last, the medicine and cream seemed to have beaten the infection. Houston's wound had healed, and we were all relieved and happy.

Ken would be leaving us to fly home to Georgia for a couple of weeks, but before he left, I had a question for him.

"Ken, would you consider adopting Houston?" I asked. "I think Houston would love to live in Georgia."

"No," Ken said, shaking his head. "I already have three dogs, and if I brought another one home, my wife would kill me."

He stood there holding Houston in his arms, petting him around his ears. I could tell he was torn and would have adopted Houston if it were possible.

"Not even a dog as cute as Houston?" I teased him. "You could tell her he barks with a drawl, and you just could not resist that southern bark."

"Not even with a barky drawl," he laughed. "I am hoping by the time I come back, he will be adopted to a nice home."

Ken left the next morning without Houston. Now that Houston was well, we all started preparing him for adoption.

A week after Ken left, he sent us a text telling us his company had moved him to another project and he would not be returning. He thanked us for letting him be a part of our shelter life and said he would miss his days spent with Houston.

We were going to miss Ken and told him we would keep him informed of how Houston was doing.

We posted Houston on our website with his picture and described him as a jaunty, lighthearted fellow who was very good with people. We had many applications on him and soon chose a home for him. His new person, who we called Miss Janey, was a patron of the shelter and had supported us for many years. Miss Janey had adopted dogs from us several times, and we knew she would make an excellent mom for Houston.

Her life had changed recently with the loss of her husband, and we knew Houston's sunny disposition would help her with her grief. She fell in love with him the moment she laid eyes on him, and Houston loved her. We texted Ken immediately with the news, and he replied with congratulations and good wishes.

For the next two weeks, we received phone calls from Miss Janey with adulation and flattery on her new boy.

Then one day on my day off, I was surprised to get a message from Emmi.

"Houston, we have a problem," she said. "I will text you when I know more."

I could not imagine what could have gone wrong, and my thoughts were going wild. I wondered if he had bitten someone or if he was too energetic for Miss Janey. Did he tear up her furniture or curtains, or was Miss Janey sick?

I thought of the wound but quickly sent it to the back of my mind. An hour later, Emmi texted me back, and my heart sank.

"Houston is back and is very sick," she texted. "I have isolated him in your office."

I could not believe it and was anxious to get back to work to see him.

The next morning, I walked through the shelter doors to be greeted by an anxious staff.

"Emmi has taken Houston back to the vet this morning," Pat said in a discouraged voice.

"What happened, and how sick is he?" I inquired.

"He is very sick," Pat informed me. "The wound has opened again and is draining. He just lies around and seems to be running a fever. Miss Janey told us he was fine the first couple of weeks, but a few days ago he became lethargic and stopped eating.

"When she called the shelter, Emmi asked her to check where the wound had been. Miss Janey felt around it and said it seemed painful for him and that it was open and starting to ooze.

"Emmi asked Miss Janey to bring him over to the shelter so she could see him. When Miss Janey got here, she was crying and told Emmi she could not take another loss right now. She felt we could give him better care, and she needed to release him back to us."

"Poor Miss Janey," I said. "Does she not want him back once he is well?"

"No," Pat sighed.

We all waited anxiously for Emmi to return, and when she did, she went straight into our director's office with Houston. After a few minutes, Emmi came to the door and asked me to come in. When I entered the office, I could tell by their sober faces it was not good news.

"Not a good report?" I said as I sat down heavily.

Emmi shook her head.

"The vet thinks the infection has spread throughout his body and feels Houston is too sick to get well. She thinks it would be more humane if Houston were euthanized."

Saddened, my heart sank, and I felt tears well up. After all he had been through, it was disappointing to think this would be the end result. It was unthinkable.

We jumped when our director slammed her fist down on the desktop.

"No," she yelled loudly.

Emmi and I both looked at her, surprised.

"When is Dr. Vincent getting back?" she demanded.

"He is supposed to get back tomorrow," Emmi said.

"Go call his wife and see if he will call me as soon as he is back," she said. "Tell her it is an emergency, and we need a second opinion."

Emmi left the room to call Dr. Vincent's wife. Houston looked so miserable as he lay on our director's lap. She gently petted him as if trying to push life into his weakened body and encourage him to live, but it was obvious he was dying, and I was frightened for him.

After a few minutes, Emmi opened the door.

"Dr. Vincent is back and will come by to pick up Houston in an hour," she said with a smile of relief.

"Oh, good," our director sighed. "We will cross every bridge we can before having him euthanized."

I was glad Dr. Vincent was back and eager for him to arrive to examine Houston. Not only was he a wonderful veterinarian with professional knowledge in veterinary medicine, but he also had a sixth sense with animals, speaking their language. He loved them, and it was evident in the way he treated and handled them.

A true scientist in his field, he had helped us to solve many mysteries, but at times he had to be the quiet voice gently guiding us to let them go. It only happened after everything had been done and they were suffering, with no quality of life left and no chance they would get well.

We completely trusted him and knew that if anyone could solve Houston's problem, it would be him.

When I got up to leave my director's office, I looked back. Houston was still lying on her lap, and tears were rolling down her cheeks, dropping onto his coat.

Dr. Vincent arrived early, and we took him into the director's office to examine Houston. After a few minutes, he asked for a towel, wrapped it around Houston, and picked him up to leave.

"I am taking him to the clinic," he said. "I will call you as soon as I know what is going on with this little guy."

We all expected to hear from him later in the afternoon, but as the hours ticked by, no word came. We stayed close to the front counter, quickly answering the phone every time it rang.

When the day ended with no news, we left to go home disappointed and worried.

I was the first to arrive at the shelter the next morning. As I was preparing for the new day, I noticed Dr. Vincent's car turn into the parking lot. He was holding Houston when he got out of his car, so I ran to the front door to hold it open for him.

He walked up to the front counter, and smiling, he slapped a plastic bag down on the countertop.

"What is that?" I asked, picking up the bag to examine it.

"What does it look like?" he asked.

I turned it over and over in my hand, looking at the object in the bag. It was black, about five inches long and a half inch wide, and both ends were rounded.

"It looks like a piece of metal," I said, still looking at it closely.

Then my eyes grew big as I realized that whatever this thing was, it was connected to Houston.

"That," he said, pointing, "is a popsicle stick."

I looked back down at the object in the bag, and even though it was black, it was a popsicle stick.

Stunned, I asked him, "Did he swallow it?"

My mind was racing because I knew animals will swallow things and the object can become an obstruction in their stomachs or intestines.

"No. I took X-rays," he said, pointing at the bag. "The X-rays showed an object was lodged behind his right shoulder down toward his rib cage, so I did surgery last night to remove it, and that is what I found."

I turned the plastic bag over in my hand, looking at the popsicle stick, wondering how on earth it could have lodged itself inside Houston's body.

I looked up at Dr. Vincent in disbelief.

"How did it get there?" I asked.

"Someone impaled him with it," he said, disgusted.

I sucked in my breath, dropping the bag on the counter. Dr. Vincent pulled out an X-ray, holding it up to the light for me to see. Sure enough, there was the popsicle stick lodged behind his right front leg, slanting down toward his rib cage.

I felt sick to my stomach. I had seen cruel things done to animals before, and it always horrified me how savage humans can be.

"You mean someone did this on purpose?" I said sadly.

He shook his head before speaking.

"Well, it looks that way. But the good news is, he will be fine now that it has been removed. With a couple of weeks of recuperation, he will be ready for his new home."

I looked at Dr. Vincent closely before asking one final question.

"I just have to ask. How did so many veterinarians miss this?"

Dr. Vincent was always kind and professional, supporting his colleagues and the people he worked alongside.

"I do not know," he said, blowing out his breath. "But remember, we are humans and work long, exhausting hours, and we get tired. There will always be mysteries to solve when it comes to animals, and sometimes a colleague will step in with fresh eyes to help solve hard cases.

Each veterinarian who treated Houston had his best

interest at heart, and if the same vet had seen him each time, they may have discovered what I found."

He handed Houston over to me. Then, showing me his staples, he reached inside his pocket, pulling out more topical cream and papers on wound care.

"I will check on him in a couple of days and then come by in fourteen days to remove the staples," he said. "I talked with your director last evening, and she knows how things turned out. Make sure you show her the popsicle stick and X-ray."

Of course, I was going to show her the popsicle stick and X-ray. Plus, I was going to show them to every staff member who walked through the doors that morning. The popsicle stick would go into our strange collection of things that showed up on or inside animals who entered our facility.

"Thank you, Dr. Vincent," I said.

Reaching over, he petted Houston on the head. Then, smiling at both of us, he waved goodbye.

Everyone was shocked to see what had been inside Houston but happy to know he would now make a full recovery. Emmi sent a text message to Ken in Georgia. He was appalled at what he read but so happy the mystery was solved and that Houston would soon be well.

Houston recovered quickly, and the quip of "Houston, we have a problem" was only said when he did something naughty. Fully recovered, he once again became his happy, jolly self, charming all the visitors who were looking for a new dog.

One day, a man in his fifties approached the front desk. He wore tweed pants and a white cashmere sweater. A seafaring cap covered his curly grey hair, making him look very dashing. He looked at us from under thick, bushy eyebrows, and his green eyes twinkled in a good-natured smile.

"Halo," he said in a Scottish brogue. "Me name be Gregor Kirk, and I want ta find out aboot the natty Schnauzer in the dog kennels," he continued in his Scottish brogue. "Ee's a fine fella, he tis."

We spent the next twenty minutes telling Mr. Kirk about Houston's wonderful personality and the incident of the popsicle stick.

"Well then," he said, "I would like ta take im for a wee walk."

Emmi went to get Houston and walked with them around the shelter grounds. When they came back in, she placed them in an adoption room so they could spend time together.

We stood at the half door listening, enchanted by his charming brogue as he lavished attention on Houston.

After a short time, Mr. Kirk looked at Emmi and questioned her.

"How do ye think e would do on a boot?"

"A boot?" she said, puzzled.

"Well," he said, "tis really more of a yacht. It tis rather big, and e would ave plenty of space ta run in."

"Oh, a yacht," she said, now smiling.

"Ooh, tis a big 'un, me boot tis," he expounded. "Do ye think e likes the wa-er, because that tis where I live, on me yacht."

"Well, I think he would adjust fine," Emmi said, laughing.

"Well then, I op so, because I think e is a fine laddy and would make a gurat first mate."

We all agreed that Houston would make Mr. Kirk a great first mate. We adopted Houston to him that day and sent him to his new home on a yacht.

Later in the fall, we received a letter with a note and picture inside from a town in the Caribbean. Houston, now renamed Gavin, was seated on a deck chair with Gregor Kirk next to him. Both of them looked smug and happy, and we all gathered together to admire the picture and read the note.

To all me friends at the Humane Society from yer sea traveling friends. Gregor calls me his first mate, and I ave got me sea legs now. He says I be a rather fiesty twit while guarding me new home. I seem ta be quit a brawler with any person I may think tis trying ta pirate me yacht. Gregor tis a fine fellow, loves drinking scotch and smoking cigars. E's a good man ta live with and has learnt ta take gurat care of me. I eat well and ave free run of me yacht. I am very appy and love me new life. Thank ye, fer introducing me ta Gregor, I am appy an well.

Yer friends, Gavin and First Mate, Gregor Kirk.

We were overjoyed to see a healthy Houston (Gavin) on deck, as he sat next to his captain with a beautiful sun setting behind them. Both were looking at us from beneath bushy eyebrows and sporting grey beards, looking well-groomed and debonair.

Two mates, happily sailing the world together.

Every dog must have it's day.

JONATHAN SWIFT

PETUNIA

IT WAS rare for a Pug to come into the shelter. When one did, we received a lot of interest, because they were sought after. Pugs are a small dog breed. Short and stocky, they have muscular chest and sturdy legs. Their heads are round, with black, wrinkled faces and squashed noses. Because their nose is squashed, they have a harder time breathing, and they make a guttural "kakr, kakr" sound as they breathe in and out. Their dark, prominent eyes are round and protrude from a black face, creating an inquisitive look of surprise. The wrinkled lines on their forehead run from the base of their nose, moving upward between their black ears. Their ears push out away from their foreheads with a slight lift. This completes their lively face, giving them an impish and mischievous look. They have short, thick coats, which can be silver, black, or fawn colored. Their tails make a perfect curl over the base of their back and only relax when they are sleeping, not feeling well, or frightened. By nature, they are little clowns and will show off for anyone who encourages them. Running with sheer joy, they do zoomies while ducking and dodging around everything in their way. They are affectionate, friendly, confident, and opinionated, knowing what they want. This makes them great pets for any household.

I was excited when I came to work one morning to hear a Pug had come in. Throwing my coat over the back of my office chair, I hurried to the small dog area to take a peek. I became alarmed and my excitement shattered when I looked inside the kennel. To my astonishment, a skeletal little Pug stood in front of me. Her body was emaciated, and she hung her head as she rocked back and forth on her little legs.

"Her name's Petunia," Heather said from behind me.

I turned to look into Heather's sad blue eyes and then back at this starved little Pug.

"She looks so pitiful," I said. "What is wrong with her?"

"She came in last evening," Heather said, stepping up next to me. "We have called Dr. Vincent, and he will come in sometime today to see her."

We stood outside Petunia's kennel, feeling sorry for her. I tapped on the window to see if she would respond. She stood swaying, trying to lift her head. Her sad, miserable eyes seemed to plead with me, asking for help. I opened the kennel door and wrapped her in a blanket. Cuddling her in my arms, I took her into my office and sat down on the floor. Adjusting the blanket on my lap, I tried to make her more comfortable. Heather had followed me in and sat on my office chair.

"What happened to her?" I asked.

"Her owner died," Heather answered. "The woman's son lives in another state. When he could not reach his mom by phone, he called the police to do a welfare check. The police found her deceased and found Petunia on the bed beside her."

"Oh no," I said, hugging her tight. "You poor little thing."

Heather continued. "They thought the woman had been dead for about ten days. Water was found, but no food. They were not sure how long the woman had been ill, and they were concerned she had not been able to care for Petunia before she died."

Heather stood up and walked over to a cabinet to get a can of wet dog food. Opening it, she put some on her finger and placed it in front of Petunia's nose for her to smell. Petunia pushed her head forward to smell Heather's finger, licked it a couple of times, and then turned her head away.

"We have been trying to get her to eat since she came in," Heather said. "But she is not interested."

She wiped her finger off and set the open can down on my desk.

"Have you called animal control to see if they noticed what kind of food she ate in her home?" I asked. "Maybe just the smell of her own food will stimulate her appetite."

"Yes, she brought some with her," Heather responded. "That is what I just tried to feed her."

"Will the family take her?" I wanted to know.

"No." Heather shook her head. "There is only one son, and he claims to be allergic to dogs."

Picking Petunia up, I looked into her wrinkled face.

"My friend, we have to find a way to get you to eat."

We are always problem-solving at the shelter, and my thoughts were rapidly turning over how we could help her.

"Have you talked to the director? Maybe we should place her in a foster home."

"We have not talked about that yet," Heather said. "We need to see what Dr. Vincent finds out. There might be other things going on with her besides a lack of food."

Heather got up to leave.

"Do you mind keeping her with you today? Maybe you could work some of your magic and get her to eat."

"Yes, I will try," I said, petting Petunia.

After Heather left, I tucked the blanket around her and placed her on a dog bed next to my chair. Picking up the can of dog food, I placed a small amount in a bowl and set it down next to her. She lifted her head to smell and then turned her head away, ignoring it.

"Come on, Petunia, you need to eat," I pleaded.

She nestled deeper into the blanket and sighed. Reaching down, I picked her back up, placing her on my lap. She curled into a tight ball and went to sleep.

Several times during the day I offered her food, but after a few licks she was done and laid her head back down. Late in the afternoon, Dr. Vincent knocked on my door and stepped in, followed by Heather.

"Is this our girl?" he asked.

Reaching down, he carefully picked her up and set her on his lap to examine her. When he was done, he slipped his stethoscope back into his coat pocket and sat back to hear her story. Heather told him how animal control had discovered Petunia and what we had been trying to do for her since she had arrived at the shelter.

"We need to get some nutrients into you, my girl," he said, petting her wrinkled head. "I need to take her to the clinic and run a blood panel," he told us. "She needs some IV fluids to get her rehydrated, and hopefully she will feel better. I may also need to do an MRI to make sure there is no underlying problem. Would it be okay with your director?"

"Yes," Heather replied. "Our director has okayed anything you need to do."

"Okay then." He stood and wrapped Petunia in the blanket. "I will take her over to the clinic and will call you as soon as I know what is going on with her."

As he carried her out to his truck, her little black face looked out from beneath the blanket.

"Goodbye, Miss Petunia," I said, touching her soft ears. "You are in good hands now."

Dr. Vincent smiled at me.

"Have you ever heard the term cuddlepugged?"

"No, I have not heard that one." I smiled back.

"It means when you cuddle with a Pug and hear its soft groans. You fall in love with them because you have been cuddlepugged," he said.

"Well, that is a great word and very fitting," I laughed.

With a confident smile, he started the truck and waved goodbye.

Cuddlepugged, I thought later. Yes, I knew this to be true, because when my son and his wife were first married, they brought a Pug puppy into their home. I could not stay away and would hurry through our evening meals so I could go cuddle with their newest family member, Ole. As I held him, he would snuggle into my neck, making the cutest baby moans. Once he found a cozy spot, he went to sleep, softly snoring. His little curled-up tail would relax and go limp. When he woke, he would stretch and make more sweet Puggy sounds. Then he would fall back asleep, limp in my arms. It was like holding a human baby, and I was in love. So I really understood what Dr. Vincent meant when he asked if I had ever been cuddlepugged. I know it is not a word in the dictionary, but it should be.

We knew Petunia was receiving the best possible care as we anxiously waited to hear from Dr. Vincent. Talking among ourselves, we worried it might be more than malnutrition that plagued her. He had her for two days before returning to the shelter. Holding her in his arms, he looked at us and shook his head.

"The only thing I can find wrong with this little dog is grief," he stated.

"Grief?" our director said, lifting her eyebrows.

Dr. Vincent shook his head, confident of his diagnosis.

"The first night I did a complete examination. I did a blood panel, MRI, and tested her for worms. They all came back negative, with no signs of disease, worms, or injuries. She felt better after the infusion and ate a few bites of wet food. I took her home with me so I could feed her every two hours. When it was time to go to sleep, Mellie insisted we tuck her in bed beside us. I got up several times during the night to see if she would eat, but she would only take a few bites."

He wiped his hand across his forehead in frustration.

"The only thing I believe is wrong with this little dog is grief," he said, resolved. "My concern is, if she does not start eating soon, her body will begin to shut down."

We often think that our pets are not capable of feeling grief, but I know this not to be true. After working for years with animals, it is obvious that they grieve. When I started working at the shelter, I had to deal with animals being left behind by their owners. They would often go into depression, and some would refuse to eat. In one incident, a tragic accident killed several family members. Animal control brought their two dogs to the shelter. They were in our care until arrangements could be made for another family member to come and get them. The female lay on her bed despondent, while the male wailed for several days. Animals feel; they feel deeply, and I knew we had to find a way to help Petunia.

"Should we put her in foster care?" our director asked Dr. Vincent.

"Well, I have been thinking about that, and I may have a

plan," he said. "I know someone who might take Petunia and pull her out of her depression. I just need to convince her."

He looked at us with a sadness in his eyes and then a mischievous grin before continuing.

"I have a neighbor who lost her husband this last year, and a month later she lost her dog. She is so heartbroken and has become very depressed. Lately she has isolated herself away, and all the neighbors are very worried about her."

"Do you think she would take Petunia?" I asked.

Our director cleared her throat, trying to get our attention.

"I am a little concerned for your neighbor," she said. "Because what would happen to her if Petunia does not make it?"

Dr. Vincent looked at her confidently.

"If she would agree to take her, I know Petunia will pull through. She has a remarkable way with animals and has helped me with many cats and dogs. She is devoted to caring for them and makes her own special food. But I think most of her healing is good old-fashioned love."

I could tell Dr. Vincent had made up his mind and was intent on giving this a try.

"I will talk with her this evening when I see her, and I would like to take Petunia home with me."

"Yes, take her home," our director said. "Like you, I feel it is worth a try. If she agrees to take her, have her come to the shelter to fill out the foster paperwork."

"Of course," he said. "I hope she will come in tomorrow."

Dr. Vincent was on a mission and all but danced across the floor. We all knew if he could persuade his neighbor to take Petunia, it could be the answer for her recovery in both body and mind. Smiling, he mischievously winked at us and tucked Petunia under his arm to leave.

When Dr. Vincent arrived home with Petunia, he sat by

the window and watched for his neighbor to take her evening walk. When he could see her coming back up the lane, he tucked Petunia into his coat front and left the house for a stroll. He waved to his neighbor as she approached him.

"Good evening, Helen," he smiled. "It is a beautiful evening, isn't it?"

Helen waved and walked over to greet him.

"It is a little windy, but yes, it is a nice evening. I think spring is on its way."

Petunia had snuggled deep inside Dr. Vincent's coat, and he was gently pushing on her to get her to pop her head out.

"What have you got there?" Helen asked, looking at his wiggling coat front.

"Oh, one of my little friends," he said. "I thought she could use an evening walk."

He unzipped his coat a little, and Petunia stuck her head out to look around.

"Oh, how cute. Is this a new member of your household?" Helen questioned him.

"No. As a matter of fact, she is a patient," he said, hoping she would quiz him.

Helen bent over to look more closely. Reaching out, she touched Petunia's soft ear.

"What kind of dog is she?" she asked, smiling.

"She is a Pug," he answered her.

Dr. Vincent knew he had Helen's interest, so he unzipped his coat, pulling Petunia out.

Helen reached out to pet her soft coat.

"You are a different-looking dog," she cooed. "With all those wrinkles, you are adorable in a comical sort of way."

Straightening up, she looked intently at Dr. Vincent.

"She looks skinny. Is she ill?"

"Yes, she is very underweight," Dr. Vincent stated. "Usually, Pugs are much fatter."

"What is the matter with her?" Helen asked, looking concerned.

"She will not eat," he answered. "Her owner died, and they found her there when they did a welfare check."

"Oh, that is horrible," Helen said, tearing up.

She folded her arms in front of herself to close off the grief she felt for Petunia. Dr. Vincent knew this was the defining moment that would determine what would happen next. He hoped he could convince Helen to take Petunia into her care. So, standing quietly, he waited for her response.

"Of course she will not eat," she stated, feeling deep sympathy for Petunia. "Poor, poor little girl, you never get over the loss of a loved one."

She grabbed a handkerchief from her pocket to wipe her eyes.

"What an awful thing to happen. It is too horrible to think about."

Dr. Vincent stood there, shaking his head in agreement. He hoped she would reach out and take Petunia from him, but instead she tucked her hands deep into her pockets.

"What is her name?" she asked.

"Petunia," he told her.

"Petunia," she repeated, looking more closely at her. "Well, I hope you get well soon, Petunia."

Patting Petunia on the head, she stepped away to continue her walk home. Walking a short distance, she turned and looked back at Dr. Vincent.

"What will happen to her now?" she inquired.

Dr. Vincent walked back toward her.

"We will need to find a foster home, but it will have to be a person with experience with underweight dogs, someone who can understand the special diet she will need," he answered.

He could see Helen's interest aroused.

"Helen, would you be interested in taking Petunia? You have such a wonderful way with sick animals."

"No, no." Helen compressed her lips, shaking her head. "I cannot. I have my own heartache to bear, and I am too frail right now."

"I am so sorry I suggested it," Dr. Vincent said, patting her on the shoulder. "It was just a thought and very heartless of me."

Helen smiled up at him.

"It is not your fault. I just need to get through this."

She moved around him and continued walking down the road. Dr. Vincent watched her walk away, and tucking Petunia deep inside his coat, he whispered,

"Petunia, let us go home and let Helen sleep on it tonight."

Whistling, he strolled back toward home.

He had finished his first cup of coffee the next morning when his phone rang. He let it ring a few times before answering.

"Good morning," he answered.

"Dr. Vincent?" the voice on the phone said. "This is Helen. How is Petunia doing this morning?"

"Oh, about the same," he said, with a grin on his face. "Still not eating much."

"Well, what are you feeding her?" her voice said, with concern.

"The best canned dog food I can find," he stated, winking at his wife, who was cooking breakfast.

"She needs a special diet," Helen said assertively.

"You are right," he smiled. "Maybe you could tell me what you would use to feed her?"

There was another silence on the other end of the phone. He took a long sip of coffee while waiting for her to respond.

"I cannot get her off my mind and thought about her all night," she said.

After another long pause, he heard her sigh.

"I think I should bring her home."

Dr. Vincent sat quietly, stirring his coffee, the spoon making a tink, tink, tink sound on the side of his cup.

"Dr. Vincent?" Helen said anxiously.

"Well, Helen, I do not know," he said, adding another spoonful of sugar. "Are you sure? It would be a lot for you to take on."

"Oh, I would really like to try," she said anxiously. "I may be the only chance Petunia has."

Dr. Vincent took another long sip of his coffee. Setting his cup down in front of him, he looked at the dark liquid in his cup and grinned.

"Well, if you think you are up to it," he said, with a voice that was still unsure. "You understand that Petunia's recovery may take a while, and of course I would have to arrange it with the shelter."

"Please, Dr. Vincent, let me try. I think it is her only hope, and it would be good for both of us," Helen pleaded.

"Well," he said, as if he were still thinking about it. "I will call the shelter and make the arrangements. I would like them to meet you, and you would need to sign some paperwork."

He took another sip of his coffee.

"Would that be okay with you?"

"Yes, that would be perfect," she said, with relief in her voice. "Let me know what time."

"I will call you back," he said. "Thank you, Helen."

Dr. Vincent hung up the phone and sat back in his chair, stretching out his long legs.

"You scoundrel," Dr. Vincent's wife said, turning a pancake on the grill.

Dr. Vincent scooped Petunia off the dog bed beside his chair and placed her on his lap.

"Well, we do what we have to do," he laughed.

Moving his hand down Petunia's wrinkled back, he took another sip of his coffee.

"Petunia, my girl," he said. "I think I may have found a home for you."

Dr. Vincent called our director, told her the news, and made arrangements for Helen to come to the shelter for us to meet her. He arrived with Petunia around one o'clock and told us how he had persuaded Helen to take Petunia.

"I have known Helen for years," he happily assured us. "She has a wonderful way with dogs."

We were all relieved for Petunia and excited to meet her new foster mom. Heather and I were the first to greet her when she arrived. Her appearance startled me, and I looked toward Heather to see what her reaction was. Unkempt would be the best description I could give. She was around the age of sixty; her hair had not been brushed, and it hung limply down her shoulders. She wore stained and dirty sweats under her unzipped coat. She wore old, torn sneakers with missing shoelaces on her feet. She greeted us with a lethargic hand-shake and a melancholy smile. Her whole appearance seemed despondent, depressed, and gloomy. The rest of the staff had gathered and were looking at Dr. Vincent, unsure. By their silence, I could tell they did not feel comfortable with the foster home he had chosen for Petunia. I smiled my way into our director's office, shutting the door behind me.

"What is up?" she asked after seeing the look on my face.

"I am hesitant about Dr. Vincent's choice of a foster," I said, concerned.

"Dr. Vincent has never steered us wrong before," she said. "I trust his judgment."

"You need to come and meet this lady," I told her.

She pushed her chair back from the desk and stood up. We walked together into the front lobby, and I could see from her expression that she too was not sure. Holding out her hand, she introduced herself to Helen.

"You must be Helen?" she said, shaking her hand.

Dr. Vincent stood behind Helen, beaming. Seeing our hesitation, he pointed toward the director's office, indicating he wanted to talk with us. Our director took Helen into an office so that she could fill out the paperwork. Walking back toward her office, she waved Dr. Vincent in.

"Julie, I want you and Heather in my office also," she told us.

When we were all seated, Dr. Vincent cleared his throat.

"I know how this must look to you," he said. "Helen is the neighbor I was telling you about."

Looking at each of us, he continued. "I know she looks awful, but this is not normal for her, which is why I have been concerned. Normally she is very neat and tidy, but with the loss of her husband and then her dog, she seems to have fallen apart."

He pulled a hanky from his pocket to clean his glasses.

"She has a wonderful way with dogs, and I know she could pull Petunia through."

He sat quietly, waiting for our response.

"I know grief is horrible," our director said in a sad voice. "But I am a little uncertain about this."

While she thought, the room remained silent. She finally cleared her throat and looked at Heather and me.

"What are you two thinking?" she asked. "Should we give Helen a chance with our little Petunia?"

The silence was deafening as we sat in our own thoughts. When she started tapping her pen on her desktop, we knew she wanted a response from us.

"I think it may be worth a try," I said. "Sometimes when people fall off the edge, they need help to claw their way back up. So maybe the two of them can help each other find their way back."

I looked around the room at each person.

"Yes, I agree," Heather said. "She may fall in love with Petunia and end up adopting her."

"That was my thought also," our director said. "It might be a lovely ending for the both of them."

Dr. Vincent released his breath.

"That is what I am hoping for, and I live right down the road from Helen, so I could check in on them a couple of times a week."

We were now more comfortable with our decision, but only because we trusted Dr. Vincent and felt confident in his judgment. Waving goodbye, Dr. Vincent stood next to us as we watched Petunia leave that day with Helen. We wished them well and hoped for a full recovery for both of them.

Our director was in weekly contact with Helen, and when Dr. Vincent was at the shelter, he would brag about how well Petunia was doing. She was gone for a month before Helen brought her to the shelter for a visit. When she walked in with her, we were astonished and amazed at the changes they both had made. Petunia was no longer scrawny and gaunt, but now she was a plump, roly-poly Pug. Her lackluster coat was healthy with a shine. A month ago, her tail hung limp behind her, but now it was curled up over her back. She was interested in her surroundings and looked curiously at us from her dark, round eyes. When Helen set her down on the floor, Petunia ran with enthusiasm and joy. Playfully, she ducked and dodged around things, zipping around the room. We laughed as she showed her happiness, and we were pleased that she looked healthy.

We were also amazed to see the changes in Helen. Her clothes were clean and fit well, complementing her trim figure. She wore makeup, and a bob haircut flattered her angular face. She greeted each of us with a confident handshake and a smile. Clapping her hands with delight, she laughed as she encouraged Petunia in her silly, ecstatic run.

"I cannot tell you what a blessing Petunia has been to me," she said, laughing.

We could see how different and happy she was as she watched Petunia with joy and love. Then, patting her leg, she encouraged her to jump onto her lap. Petunia sat panting as she looked into Helen's face with adoration.

"She looks so healthy," Heather said, smiling.

"She does," Helen said proudly, looking down at Petunia. "All it took was a little love and some good food."

Her face clouded for a moment before she spoke again.

"Now that she is healthy, I know I will have to return her soon."

She petted Petunia's back, moving her hand up around her ears.

"She has been really good for me," she said.

Hearing Helen from her office, our director came out to see Petunia.

"Wow, you both are looking well," she said, admiring the change in them. "Dr. Vincent has kept me informed about Petunia, and I think you should consider adopting her."

Helen sat silent for a moment and then started to cry.

"Are you serious?" she sniffled.

"Dead serious," our director laughed.

"I would love to, but I was afraid to ask."

Huge tears were rolling down her face, and our director handed her a tissue.

"I cannot think of a better home for her," our director said.

Helen took the tissue and wiped her eyes.

"She saved my life," Helen whispered.

"And you saved hers," our director smiled.

Petunia went home with Helen that sunny morning. In the following months, when Dr. Vincent came to the shelter, he would inform us how both Petunia and Helen were doing.

"I see them all the time when they walk in the evenings," he would say proudly. "It is a remarkable change they both have made."

With his legs stretched out in front of him, he would sit thoughtfully, reflecting.

"I do not think we understand the impact of loss and grief on animals," he said quietly. "Petunia was in such grief, and I think she would have starved to death if Helen had not intervened."

The room remained quiet for a moment before he continued.

"We humans think we know it all with our big brains, but animals understand grief. They show more empathy and tenderness toward humans than most humans show toward their animals."

Introspective, he leaned forward in his chair and looked at us.

"It was a good thing we did for Helen and Petunia, because only they could understand how each other felt."

He sat back and stared into space, lost in the memories of the last few months. Taking his glasses off, he wiped them on the front of his shirt and stood to leave. He stood there silently for a moment and then waved his glasses at us before seriously saying,

"If Mellie dies before I do, please insist I get another dog."

A dog is the only thing that can mend a crack in your broken heart.

JUDY DESMOND

O'MALLY

SOME DOGS never grow up or grow old. They love social interaction and will go to great lengths to find any opportunity to interact with another dog or a human. Such as O'Mally.

Officer Baily brought him to the shelter early one morning after she found him sprinting down the middle of the road, oblivious to cars. He was still panting as if he had never stopped running, even with the ride over to our facility.

He was a Labradoodle with a shaggy brown coat and a scruffy face. His black button eyes looked at us with excitement, ready for his next adventure. He shook his tousled and windblown coat while wagging his friendly tail.

Social and gregarious, he looked around for a new friend. He spotted Pat as she walked around the counter. Happy to meet this new person, he raced toward her. Jumping, he covered her shirtfront with his oversized paws, giving her a big slurpy kiss across her face.

"Phew," she said, wiping her face.

Officer Baily pulled the dog off. "I found him close to St. John's Catholic Church on Evergreen Street."

"Sit down, you big goofus," she said, still struggling with him.

"Friendly, isn't he?" Pat said, wiping the slobber off her shirtfront.

Officer Baily clipped our leash onto the dog's collar before slipping her leash off.

"You can release him to his owner if they come in. Email their information to me so I can contact them," she requested.

She signed the papers at the front counter and turned to leave. The dog sat watching her, his tail rapidly moving back and forth, back and forth, sweeping the floor. Once her vehicle drove away and it was no longer in sight, the dog turned his head back toward us.

Once again, he spotted Pat, who was lifting her hands in the air, trying to ward him off. Thrilled, he started bouncing on his front feet, moving toward her with excitement. Pat was our smallest staff member. Barely five feet tall and most likely weighing around ninety-eight pounds, she had the stature of a child. In this dog's opinion, she looked like a perfect playmate, and he wanted to play.

Sidestepping him, she bent to pick up his leash.

"Come on, you big oaf," Pat ordered.

Scolding him, they walked down the hall. I could tell he did not mind the dressing down he was getting from her, as he happily bounced and pranced beside her. When Pat opened the door into intake, the dog hurled himself into the room.

"Who's this?" Emmi asked, smiling.

"A goofus," Pat retorted, handing her his leash. "Watch it; he will jump on you."

She gave Emmi the information she would need and, happy to be rid of him, shut the door behind her.

The dog was delighted to be in a new space with a new person to get acquainted with. He ran around the room while

Emmi started his paperwork. She took his collar off to attach the shelter tag to it. Patting him on top of his curly head, she placed the collar back around his neck.

"I can tell you did not make a good impression on Pat," she commented.

He wiggled with sheer joy, thrilled with her touch. Then, like a distracted child, he turned to snoop around the room. Emmi reached for the microchip scanner lying on the countertop and called him over.

"Sit still for a minute," she told him as she ran the scanner over his back.

Beep, beep, beep, it sounded. Holding it up, she read the numbers and wrote them down. Picking up her radio, she asked Pat to come back to intake.

Soon Pat knocked on the door and came in. He was thrilled to see her returning, but before he could jump on her, Emmi grabbed him by the collar. Handing Pat the paper, she asked her to call the microchip company.

Pat carefully squeezed back through the door and left. When the door closed, the dog turned his full attention back to Emmi. He play bowed and barked, trying to invite her to have a friendly romp.

"You're a rowdy one," Emmi laughed. "And you sure have a cute face."

Spinning in a circle, he pounced on the ball she threw for him, grabbing it up in his mouth.

About forty-five minutes later, Pat was back with the information Emmi would need. Knocking on the intake door, she opened the door a crack and peeked in. Slipping the paper through, she yelled through the small gap, "His name is O'Mally, and he's a one-year-old neutered male."

Hearing his name, O'Mally jumped on the door and tried

to see through the small opening. Pat pushed hard against his weight, shouting the rest of his information to Emmi.

"Angus O'Brian is his owner, and he lives on the same street where they found him."

"Oh good, have you called him yet?" Emmi asked.

"Yes, I left a message on his phone."

When Pat let go of the door to leave, it slammed shut. With his front feet still firmly planted on the door, O'Mally looked curiously back at Emmi, as if to say,

"Who was that?"

Emmi laughed. "That was your good friend Pat."

After completing O'Mally's intake, Emmi walked him to the dog runs. He greeted each dog as he walked by, glad to meet them. When Emmi found an empty kennel, she filled it with toys, fresh water, food, and a nice blanket on the bed.

He zoomed around the kennel and scooped up a favorite toy. Trotting over to the bed, he lay down to play with it. Before she left, Emmi bent over him and petted him.

"I like you, even if you are a goofus," she told him.

After O'Mally's intake was done and Emmi had typed his information into the computer, the rest of the morning remained quiet.

When everyone arrived back from lunch and had prepared for their afternoon, a priest walked through the front door.

"How can I help you?" Emmi asked.

"Good day," he said in an Irish brogue. "I am Father O'Brian, and I am ere for me dog."

He smiled a congenial, pleasant smile while twisting a leash in his hands. He was a small man, and he was neatly dressed in black with a white clerical collar. His blue eyes looked at Emmi from behind round wire-framed glasses. He was mostly bald except for the band of white hair that circled the back of his head.

"Who is your dog?" Emmi asked.

"O'Mally," he said, and lowered his voice to tell her something confidentially. "He is a bit of a scoundrel and loves to run away."

"O'Mally is your dog?" Emmi said, surprised.

Father O'Brian shook his head, affirming he was the owner. Then, with a smile, he placed his right hand up with two fingers pointed toward the ceiling and made the sign of the cross.

"Every night, I ave to absolve im of his sins," he laughed.

Emmi laughed also, moving around the counter to shake Father O'Brian's hand.

"I must admit he's a bit of a handful, but he's friendly," she said.

"He is at that," Father O'Brian agreed.

Emmi laughed. "I'll do the return to owner, and then we'll get him out for you."

She typed Father O'Brian's information into the computer and then asked Pat to bring O'Mally to the front counter.

Everyone could hear them coming, as O'Mally hurled himself through the dog-wing doors. Catapulting down the hall, he pulled Pat along behind him. When he spotted Father O'Brian, he raced toward him, barking. Reaching him, he jumped up, placing both front paws on the shoulders of Father O'Brian's shirt, licking his face.

"Ye're a happy bairn, you ease," Father O'Brian smiled, grabbing his whiskered face in his hands. "Ye brute of a dog, down with ye," he ordered.

O'Mally stayed right where he was, his tail wagging, while Father O'Brian snapped the leash onto his collar.

"Thank ye," he said to Emmi, pushing O'Mally to the floor.

O'Mally excitedly whizzed around Father O'Brian's legs,

tangling the leash around them. When they finally reached the shelter doors, Father O'Brian turned and waved.

Two days later, O'Mally was back at the shelter. This time a good citizen brought him in after finding him playing with her children in the backyard. Happily, he greeted all of us as long-lost friends.

We called Father O'Brian and told him O'Mally had been brought into the shelter again. Acting surprised, he explained he would be officiating a funeral in the early afternoon but would come pick him up after four.

We put O'Mally in a front office with a window. Around noon, Officer Baily came in with another dog and some paperwork. Seeing O'Mally looking out of the office window, she walked over to it.

"Is this that damn dog again?" she asked, looking down at him.

"Yes, it's O'Mally," I answered her.

O'Mally jumped on the window. Licking and slobbering it with his tongue, he smeared it with his hairy paws.

"Did you call Father what's-his-name?" she said, tapping on the window, exciting O'Mally even more.

"You mean Father O'Brian," Emmi answered her. "Yes, he has been called."

Even more excited with her presence and the tapping on the window, O'Mally started running in big circles, bucking and jumping in the air.

"He's a crazy dog." Tap, tap, tap went her finger. "You're a wacko," Officer Baily shouted at him as she continued to tap.

"This time make Father what's-his-name come and get a release from me," she ordered. "He needs to be more responsible and keep a better eye on his dog."

O'Mally was thrilled with all the attention and started

barking at her. "Hey dumb (#**)," she yelled, tap, tap, tap. "Settle down."

We called Father O'Brian to tell him he would have to bring in a release from animal control before picking up O'Mally. Late in the afternoon, he came with the release in hand.

When O'Mally heard his voice, he started barking and jumping all over the smeared glass. Father O'Brian squinted as he tried to look through the window at him.

"Did he make that mess?" he asked, looking at us in disbelief. "He be a scoundrel, that one tis."

Emmi opened the door and grabbed O'Mally's leash before he could leap out.

"Yes, he's had a very busy afternoon housekeeping," she laughed.

Father O'Brian shook his head. "I ave to watch im closer, or Officer Baily will give me another tongue-lashing."

Emmi handed O'Mally over to Father O'Brian. Elated to be out of the room, O'Mally jerked on the leash, dragging the poor man toward the outside doors. Father O'Brian looked back toward us, waving goodbye with a calm, serene smile.

Once they were gone, Pat put her hands on her hips and sighed.

"I think that dog's too much for him," she said.

"Yes, he needs a calmer dog for his line of work," Emmi responded, and then, lifting her eyebrows, mused, "Or maybe he needs some excitement in his life."

"Well, O'Mally will certainly provide that," Pat huffed.

They both turned and looked at the office window. Emmi grabbed paper towels so she could wash O'Mally's slobber off the glass.

"I hope we don't see them again," she laughed.

"Me too," Pat said. "But I doubt it, poor man."

It was obvious that O'Mally needed a lot of stimulation and interaction to be happy. So we were not surprised three weeks later when Officer Baily once again brought him back to the shelter.

After escaping from the parsonage, he roamed the neighborhood and found some children to play with. During his morning romp with them, he came across a mud puddle and rolled in it. Even though he was caked in mud, his new little friends decided to take him home.

The children did not seem to mind that he had bathed in mud, and while they continued to play, he rolled around on the light blue carpet. When he grew tired, he made himself at home on the beige couch to take a nap while they sat on the floor watching TV.

An hour later, when their mom came home after grocery shopping, she found her children quietly sitting in the front room with a mud-caked dog sitting amongst them. Questioning her children where they had found the dog, they innocently shrugged their shoulders, telling her he had come to play.

She tried to grab his collar to pull him off her sofa, but he stubbornly planted his body into the cushions, not willing to move. Not knowing who the dog belonged to, she called animal control.

Officer Baily showed up at their home about twenty minutes later and quickly removed O'Mally. When she walked him into the shelter, she was in a sour mood. We looked down at O'Mally, and he looked back at us from beneath a mud-crusted face. The same dried mud covered his curly coat.

"He made a mess of that poor woman's home, and you should see my van," Officer Baily said in an annoyed voice.

"I can't understand how his owner can't manage to keep the son of a (&*$@#) at home."

"Hi, O'Mally," I greeted him.

"You see this mud all over him and me? Well, you should have seen her rug and furniture." Officer Baily slapped the top of the counter with her hand.

O'Mally sat in front of her, wagging his mud-dried tail, leaving a trail of dirt with each swipe. Our director walked out of her office to see what all the commotion was about.

We could tell by the look on her face she wanted the cursing to stop because visitors were coming and going. O'Mally, happy to meet a new person, tried to jump on her. I grabbed his leash and trotted him back toward the dog runs, where he would not be such a nuisance.

The last thing I heard as we went through the dog-wing door was,

"Don't bathe that dog," Officer Baily called out. "Father what's-his-name can wash him when he gets him home. Then I think he should do an exorcism and sprinkle him with holy water."

Once again, a penitent and contrite Father O'Brian came to the shelter to claim his dog. He looked at us with remorse while explaining, "Ah don't know why e won't stay ta home," he said, handing us the new release. "Officer Baily gave me a real come-upance, she did."

"I'm sorry, Father O'Brian, I know this is a real problem for you," Emmi sympathized.

"Well, I'll take im home and give it a go, the tatty fellow. He really tis a grand dog though."

Emmi left to get Father O'Brian's dog. When he saw O'Mally approaching him, caked in all the mud, he put his hands up for O'Mally to stay down, but O'Mally did not care and made a flying leap toward him.

"Bugger off, you grand pup, what's this ave been up to?"

O'Mally ignored his reprimand, wiggling with happiness at seeing his owner.

"Well, I ave to take ye home and give ye a bath," he sighed. "Come on, lad."

We called Father O'Brian several times in the coming months to see how things were going. He assured us O'Mally was staying at home after he had found a way to contain him. He also informed us that some children from his parish loved O'Mally, and he was taking him over to play with them twice a week.

Late in the summer, one of our volunteers was getting married and had invited the shelter staff to her wedding. It was an evening wedding, which was to be held at St. John's. We were all excited to attend, and on the night of the event, Pat, Emmi, and I went together.

Before the wedding started, we watched Officer Baily come in and sit in one of the pews toward the front. The bride and groom said their vows and exchanged rings. Because it was a full Mass, they would serve the sacraments.

Just before communion, a man stood to sing the Lord's Prayer. He sang with a rich baritone voice. Midway through the song, he was joined by a low wolfish howl, echoing from somewhere in the back halls of the church. As his voice became higher, so did the dog's howls.

He reached the end of the song and began to sing the final stanza. "For thine is the kingdom, the power, and the glory, forever," he sang. We could hear the howls, low and mournful, echoing and bouncing around the chambers of the church.

"Aaameeeen," the man sang, and O'Mally's howls slowly, slowly receded away.

Everyone was chuckling under their breath, except Father O'Brian. Red-faced, he tried to keep the solemnity of the sacraments. After the priest prepared the Eucharist, people began to go up to the front for communion.

Emmi nudged me and pointed. I looked over to see where she was pointing and could see Officer Baily standing up. She slowly and reverently walked to the front with her hands folded in front of her. Lifting her head, she received the bread dipped in wine. Taking a step back, she bowed her head and made the sign of the cross.

"She's Catholic," Emmi whispered, looking surprised at both Pat and me.

"Well, you could have knocked me over with a wee feather," I whispered back.

For the next week, we retold the events of the wedding and our discovery about Officer Baily. We now looked at her differently. Not so much as the hardened ex-army drill sergeant or the no-nonsense animal control officer always putting on a tough front. Now we knew she had a softer side, a hidden devout side.

Father O'Brian kept in contact with us for many months, but he finally realized O'Mally needed a home with children. He called us before Christmas to tell us he had re-homed O'Mally to one of his parishioners with seven children.

"O'Mally tis much happier in his new home," he told me over the phone.

"Yes, Father O'Brian, I think you did the right thing," I answered back.

"But, he was a grand dog though."

There was silence on the other end of the receiver for a moment, then he spoke up.

"I could not take the ire of that woman one more time, ya know," he said in a quiet voice.

"Oh, you mean Officer Baily?"

"Aye, she can put an Irish fisherman to shame with that tongue of hers," he retorted.

He must have felt remorseful and quickly ended the conversation.

In the early spring, just before the tulips started blooming, Father O'Brian came into the shelter with a small dog tucked under his arm. He held her up for us to see and admire. She was a West Highland Terrier with a white curly coat. Her eyes were black and round, and her ears pricked forward with curiosity as she wiggled her little black nose, trying to get our scent.

"Father O'Brian, where did you find this one?" I asked.

"I didn't find er, the little lass tis mine," he said, smiling.

"Oh, she's beautiful," I said, admiring her.

"This tatty girl be Bridget, and here be her microchip number in case she ever tis brought into the shelter."

He placed a piece of paper on the counter in front of me.

"Oh good," I said, picking up the paper. "I'll put it into the computer under your name."

We all held and admired Bridget while Father O'Brian looked on with pride.

Emmi whispered to me, "I think this is a much better dog for him, and she won't give him any trouble."

"I think so too," I smiled back.

It was not even a week later before Officer Baily walked through the shelter doors carrying a small white dog.

"Look at this cutie pie," she said, holding it up for us to look at.

"Oh, she is cute. Where did you find her?" Emmi asked.

"On the steps of St. John's," Officer Baily said nonchalantly, kissing the dog on the nose. "I think someone must have abandoned her there, poor baby."

"I think that's Bridget," I mused, grabbing the microchip scanner.

"You know this dog?" Officer Baily said, holding her out so I could scan her.

Beep, beep, beep, sounded the scanner. Emmi hurried to the computer to look up the numbers.

"Yup," we heard Emmi say. "It's Bridget."

"Who's Bridget?" Officer Baily asked, looking between the two of us.

"It's Father O'Brian's new dog, Bridget," I said hesitantly.

"What! That old fart got another dog?"

Emmi and I stood there, shaking our heads up and down, while Officer Baily looked at both of us in disbelief.

"I can't believe it," she said, turning her gaze on the dog. "You little turd, you managed to get away from him already."

Emmi cleared her throat. "Officer Baily, you did say you found her on the front steps of St. John's."

"Well," she said, clicking her tongue and tucking the dog under her arm. "I'm taking her over there right now, and I'm going to give him a piece of my mind."

We watched her back her van out of a parking space and hurry out of the parking lot. Emmi looked over at me with a concerned look.

"That poor man," she said. "Did you see the look on her face when we told her who the dog belonged to?"

"Yes," I said, laughing. "You could have knocked her over with a wee feather."

"Poor, poor man," Emmi said, concerned. "I think we should pray."

A dog is a bond between strangers.

JOHN STEINBECK

PRINCESS

I KNOW this may seem odd to lump a cat into my book when I have only written about dogs, but Princess deserves a chapter, and her story merits being told.

Princess was at the shelter when I arrived, tucked inside a kennel with another shelter cat named Ava. Rescuers found her as a feral kitten, and Ava mothered her into adulthood, teaching her the ropes of shelter life. As much as the staff tried to tame her, she remained aloof and skittish around people. Eventually she accepted staff, but never to the point of letting us handle her too much. She had her favorites, one being Eileen, and I would like to think she liked me also, especially because we became working partners.

She and Ava were our resident cats and had the run of the building during the day. Princess was short-haired, with a glossy black coat. She looked at you from behind intense, moon-shaped yellow eyes, which gave her a look of being spooked by something or someone. Ava, a short-haired black-and-white, had a loving personality and was never concerned with the everyday life of the shelter. She was confident with people who came to visit and, as our receptionist, was a one-cat welcoming committee.

Princess, on the other hand, was always nervous and scared of visitors. Aloof and reserved, most of the time she stayed hidden. Scurrying low to the ground, she looked for places to hide. If anyone came near her, she would run to one of her secret hidey-holes where she could look out at their passing feet. She knew she was hidden there and felt safe.

Sometimes, she would surprise us by walking up to one of us. Tail high and purring, she groomed us with affection while brushing her body alongside our legs. If we reached down to stroke her, she would scamper away. If we managed to touch her, she became indignant, and after darting a short distance from us, she grumpily licked away our scent.

We always warned visitors not to pet her because, depending on her mood, she might lash out and scratch them. Indignant at their endeavors, she gave them a haughty look of, "You don't touch the Princess."

After she was older, she would allow certain visitors to pet her. We never knew who would be permitted to make over her or who she would scratch, so our immediate reaction was to tell people to be careful, because she could be unpredictable. On those days when she was feeling cordial, and a visitor was allowed to pet and coo over her, Princess, poised and amiable, would scoff at us as if to say,

"What are you fussing and worried about? This person is nice."

Over the years, we learned she did everything based on her mood. It could be a sonnet of purrs or a painful scratch.

Princess and Ava were a part of our everyday life at the shelter, and they were a major source of stress relief for the staff. When we arrived each day, we opened their kennels to give them a morning greeting and let them run free.

Visitors asked if they were up for adoption, and we would shake our heads no as we explained to them that the shelter was their home, and they were much loved. We enjoyed their presence and companionship, and it helped visitors relax as they interacted with them. Whether they were curled up together taking a pleasant afternoon nap or sitting on the front counter, visitors loved seeing them—or at least seeing Ava.

One day we noticed Ava was not feeling well. Hunched up in her kennel, she refused to come out and would not eat or drink. We gathered around her, worried, while Heather called the vet clinic. Dr. Vincent could see her, so Heather gently placed her in a cat carrier to take her.

When she returned, we congregated around her to hear what was ailing Ava, but it was not good news. Dr. Vincent had found a mass and told Heather Ava would not be with us for long.

Over the next couple of weeks, we nurtured her with love. When the day came for her to leave us, we cried.

After she was gone, we watched Princess grieve as she searched for Ava everywhere. Her world had changed with a major part of her security gone. She became despondent and was more nervous than ever, hiding during the day. No matter how we tried to comfort her, she remained miserable.

It broke our hearts because we did not have the knowledge to help her. Someone suggested we get another companion cat for her, and after talking amongst ourselves, we decided it should be a kitten.

It was not kitten season, so while we waited, we gave Princess a new and bigger home. We had a huge parrot cage that was almost floor to ceiling. Scrubbing it clean, we then put all Princess's things inside and rolled it in front of the window, where she could see out.

In that part of the shelter, Princess could watch what was going on in the outdoor world while still feeling safe. The whole time we cleaned, she suspiciously watched us but never offered to go in. After everything was in place, we tried to entice her to check out her new accommodations, but she refused.

We tempted her with kitty treats, wet food, a comfortable bed, toys, and a hammock bed to swing in. She sat watching us from a distance, not acting interested, and turning her head away, she snubbed our efforts.

Eileen, our cat person, watched all our attempts at luring and coaxing Princess and finally told us to leave her alone and let nature take its course.

"Cats," she said, "are curious by nature, and the minute we are gone, she will go inside to investigate."

She was right. The next morning when we came to work, Princess was inside her new kitty apartment, curled up on the soft bed, purring and peaceful.

She loved her new house and sat happily on the shelf or luxuriated in her hammock while looking outdoors. We were delighted to hear her soothing purrs while she tranquilly massaged the side of her bed with her front feet. She seemed happy and content, so content that we forgot to look for another cat.

Princess loved her new plushy pad and became very attached to it.

One day, our director moved it across the lobby in front of the other window. Princess, finicky and fussy, was not happy and threw a yowling feline fit.

Unhappily, she confronted us the moment we came in each morning, following us around, crying out her despair and frustration. This went on for about a week before I could no longer stand it, and with Eileen's help, we dragged and pulled the huge kennel back across the room to its original spot.

Princess jumped in, gave herself a bath, snuggled deep into her bed, and took a long-deserved nap. She slept for two days, which told us she must have been up most of the night worrying.

When our director finally noticed Princess's apartment back in its original place, she gave us a suspicious look.

"That's odd; I thought we moved Princess's kennel to the other window," she said with a puzzled look.

"We did," Eileen stated. "But she followed us around all day, stressed and crying. She was so unhappy that I felt sorry for her, so we moved it back."

Eileen was always an agreeable person. She never made waves or fussed about anything, but Princess's happiness was where she was going to take a stand. With her hands on her hips and an unwavering look, she stood her ground.

Our director looked at all of us, and then down at Princess, and her face softened.

"Miss Princess, did you not like where I put your kennel?" she asked with a smile.

Princess looked up at her, stretched, and tucked her head back down into her curled-up body.

"Hum," was the only sound our director made as she turned and walked into her office, shutting the door behind her.

Princess's apartment was never moved again—well, only slightly. When we put up the Christmas tree each year, we had to move her kennel a few feet to set the tree up. Visitors could see the lighted tree as they turned into our parking lot.

I really think Princess thought we put the tree there for her. Reaching out between the bars, she would bat at the hanging ornaments or lay beneath it during the day. It was another good place to hide and scare the dogs or people as they passed by. We enjoyed her holiday fun, but I think the dogs thought of her as a grinch with claws.

I do not know when she decided she needed a job. Or maybe it was out of boredom or orneriness, but it was not long before I had a new partner with my dog evaluations.

One morning when I walked a dog through the front doors, Princess made her presence known. As we entered the building, she hissed, humped up her back, fluffed out her tail, and sauntered sideways toward us on stiff legs. I stopped dead in my tracks, wondering if she was serious and if she had full intentions of attacking the dog at the end of my leash.

The dog was frightened and, taking no chances, turned to run back through the doors we had just entered. At first I thought it was just a fluke, and Princess happened to have been there at that moment, but the next day she was back and waiting. Once again, she tried to scare the dog at my side as we entered the building.

I avoided the situation, backing out the door, and talked with Emmi about it.

"Have you seen what Princess is doing when I come through the front doors with a dog?" I asked Emmi.

"No, what is she doing?" She responded nonchalantly.

I told her about the recent encounters I was having when bringing a dog through the front doors.

"I'll have to watch," she said, laughing.

Soon all the staff were watching and laughing. After observing one of my encounters, Heather noticed Princess was only doing it to me during evaluations and not anyone else who was coming in with a dog.

"What do you mean?" I questioned her after she told me.

"I've been watching," she said. "When animal control, the public, or volunteers bring a dog in, she ignores them."

"You're kidding?" I said, looking over at Princess.

"No, I'm not," she smiled matter-of-factly. "She doesn't do it with anyone else who is here with a dog, just you."

I must have had an unbelieving expression on my face, because she challenged me.

"Go get a dog," she laughed. "You'll see."

I went to the kennels to get a dog out and bring him up front. Before I had come close to the front counter, Princess had heard me and positioned herself behind it. Like a cunning combatant, she was ready to pounce.

The dog I was bringing had already had an unpleasant experience with her, so when he noticed her, he tried to get away from the cat who was waiting for him. I spun around to take him back to his kennel. As we went back through the dog-wing doors, he looked back to make sure Princess was not behind him.

That day, Princess became my working partner after I realized she had every intention of helping me with my evaluations.

I knew I could depend on her to let me know if a dog was cat friendly, frightened of cats, chased them for fun, or chased to kill a cat. I could also test their recall to see if they would listen to me when I tried to call them back, or if they would ignore the command to leave and continue with the chase.

Princess was having the time of her life, becoming very proficient and skilled at her job. When she heard me coming, she would position herself behind walls, doors, or high on a shelf. She got very good at telling if a dog was cat aggressive and seemed to know how to gauge her timing with a hiding spot in mind where she could run for safety.

If she became tired of waiting and thought I was not using my time punctually, she would stroll by my door, meowing to get my attention. It worked every time, and the dog I was evaluating would alert me and run to the door to let me know a cat was in the hallway—or they would ignore her.

Princess's inventiveness and creativity continually amazed me, as she consistently created new plans of action to test the dogs.

Several years after working together, Princess heightened the drama. One day when I walked into the building, she jumped sideways at us and chased us down the hall.

I spent the next couple of years running from Princess, pulling the dogs after me—or being pulled by the dogs—as we tried to get away from her. If I knew a dog was cat aggressive, I would try to spot where Princess was hiding when I entered the building or walked down the hall. Once I spotted her, I would yell for help from the staff so they could shoo Princess from her hiding place before she could jump out at us.

Over the years she never caught one of the dogs as we ran from her, and I do not know what she would have done if she had, but I have a pretty good idea.

Princess was my colleague and accomplice for around eight years. She loved her job and took her responsibilities seriously. It gave her purpose in life, and she was a valued member of our staff.

After an encounter with her, I would know if a dog should go to a home where cats lived or if they should be in a home minus cats. Either way, we had very few incidents of dogs being returned because of a cat issue.

Princess would delight or scare visitors with her behavior. Wide-eyed, they watched Princess chase me and the dogs down the hall. When they questioned the staff about it, they were told Princess was part of the shelter workforce and helped me with dog evaluations.

Some people thought it was cruel, but what they did not

understand was that Princess loved her job and would have thrown a tantrum if she could not participate.

In all the years she helped me, it amazed me she never outright attacked any dog. Some people would say she was getting her bluff in, but I think she got her jollies out of it.

After scaring and intimidating a dog, she sat grooming herself. It was as if she scratched her claws on her shoulder and then admired her nails while she blew on them. It was a great joke to her, and she got a lot of fun out of it.

She loved her line of work, and it gave her purpose. She did not hunt mice; she hunted dogs.

One morning when I arrived at work, Eileen anxiously met me at the door.

"I don't think Princess is feeling well," she said, with worry lines on her forehead.

I walked over to her kennel and looked in. She lay curled up on her bed in a tight ball.

"Hey, Princess," I said. "Are you okay?"

Looking up at me, she laid her head back down. I bent over and leaned in to pet her. She allowed me to touch her but did not move. Her body was stiff and cool, and I carefully picked her up. This was the first time I had ever held her since I had been at the shelter.

"See, she doesn't care if someone is touching her," Eileen remarked, her voice breaking.

When staff arrived to start the new day, we all stood around Princess's kennel, anxiously looking down at her. Emmi arrived and noticed us gathered there.

"What's up?" she said, concerned, as she laid her belongings on the front counter.

"Princess is not acting well," I stated.

Emmi reached in to pet Princess and gently handled her. After a few minutes, she walked toward the phone.

"I'll call Dr. Vincent," she said.

While she was on the phone with him, we went through all the scenarios of what could be wrong. Like everyone with a sick pet, we questioned each other.

"Could she have eaten something?"

"Maybe it was a cold. Did she have her shots this year?"

"Has she injured herself somehow?"

"Was the food she has been eating bad?"

The staff questioned, evaluated, and sought out everything.

When Emmi walked back toward us and said, "Get a crate. I'll take her to the clinic," Eileen went to the next room to get a carrier and put a soft blanket inside.

We took the top off the carrier, and Emmi gently lifted Princess to place her inside. I snapped the top on, and Emmi left with her.

We felt relieved as we watched them leave and were glad that Dr. Vincent could see her. We knew we needed to go about our daily chores, and throughout the morning we waited anxiously for news on how Princess was doing.

Emmi returned later in the morning and told us Dr. Vincent would run tests on her and bring her home at the end of his workday.

Late in the afternoon he arrived with Princess. While gently laying her in her kennel, he told us he would call with the results of her tests in a couple of days.

"If you have any concerns before then, call me," he said.

During the next couple of days, Princess improved some, but she was still not herself. As we waited for Dr. Vincent's report, we doted on her, trying to nurse her back to health.

We coaxed her with her favorite wet food and kept notes on any signs of improvement. She moved stiffly around but mainly lay on her bed, sunning herself in the warm sun. It gave us hope maybe she was on the mend, but when the reports came back, we were disappointed and grieved.

"Princess has cancer," Dr. Vincent said, looking at us sympathetically.

"The reason her belly is distended is because it's in her stomach," he said, shaking his head sadly. "There is nothing I can do for her, but I'll try to make her comfortable."

Some of us cried while others stood around, shocked.

"Is she in pain?" our director asked.

"It is hard to tell, but the way she is acting, my guess is yes," he said.

We all talked together and came to the agreement that we could not allow our girl to suffer.

We agreed not to send Princess back to the clinic and planned for Dr. Vincent to return in the evening after most of us had left for the day. Our director closed the shelter so we could have the day to ourselves and say our goodbyes.

As sad as this was, Princess had a good life, and I think it is important that we grieve when we have the loss of a pet.

As we love people, we also love our pets, and to lose one leaves a deep wound in our hearts. With all grief, it takes time, and as time goes by, the wonderful things about our loved ones surface, bringing us joy in their memories.

Memories are a significant part of our lives, making us who we are with a human capacity to love and the animals' capacity to love us back. With the pets we have in our lives, they bring us joy, laughter, and yes, in the end, tears.

Princess brought us all of that. Her presence was comforting and cherished.

After her passing, there was a vital part of our shelter life missing. Her moon-shaped yellow eyes peeking out at us from her hiding places. The memory of her lying on her hammock, sunning herself, or sitting on the front desk grooming. Her morning greetings, her joy of the Christmas tree, or that very special moment when she rubbed against our legs.

She had a quirky personality and was spooked by people she did not know and a prankster with dogs.

We have so many wonderful memories, and there will never be another Princess. She was truly a one-of-a-kind kitty.

One day we will again see our animals in the eternity of Christ.

POPE PAUL VI

A SOUL AT EASE

A leash, a path, the morning still,
A wagging tail, a gentle thrill.
Through fields and trees we find our pace,
A quiet joy, a sacred place.
No need for words, just breath and breeze,
A moment shared, a soul at ease.

THACKRAY

RALPHY BEAR

"HE LOOKS JUST LIKE A BEAR, doesn't he?" Kevin said, pointing at the dog in the kennel.

"Wow!" I agreed. "That is unbelievable; he does look like a bear."

In the kennel's corner, sitting on a bed, was a dark brown dog with a cinnamon-colored, pointed nose. His coat clung to his body and was knotted with tangled mats. His kind eyes reflected his misery as he painfully got off his bed to come over and greet us. I called to him, and he moved toward me, the heavy mats swaying on his back.

"We named him Ralphy Bear," Kevin interrupted my thoughts. "You wouldn't believe the reactions we are getting from visitors who walk by his kennel."

I agreed with Kevin; he looked exactly like a bear, bobbed tail and all. The exception was that I had never seen a bear covered with mats like these.

"Poor dog," I said, feeling distressed at the sight of him. "We need to have you groomed and get those terrible mats off."

"What kind of dog do you think he is?" Kevin asked.

"Well, I'm pretty sure he has Chow in him, but I can't be sure of the rest," I said. Inquisitively, I leaned closer for a better look.

"He may have Australian Shepherd in him as well."

We stood beside each other watching Ralphy Bear move painfully around his kennel. The mats rocked back and forth as he tried to walk.

"That is pitiful," I said, annoyed, agitated with the person who had neglected him by letting his coat get into such a terrible condition.

"Who would be so irresponsible?" I stated exasperated.

Kevin shook his head in agreement.

"I don't know, but because he came in as a stray, we can't help him until the seventy-two-hour hold is up."

When I see animals in this condition, it angers me. Animals have no choice in the homes they live in. They depend on the care of humans, who should be able to look at a dog with this kind of matting and attempt to have it groomed. I'm always surprised at how nonchalant and inhuman humans can be. What surprises me even more is how forgiving dogs are with their owners.

Mats are very painful, and a dog with long or thick hair will need to be combed daily and groomed. If it had been an emergency, we could have helped him before the hold was up, but because it was not, we would have to wait. After seventy-two hours, we could legally claim Ralphy Bear and take ownership of him. Only then could we get him help; meanwhile, it was imperative to get animal control involved.

"Is he friendly?" I asked, putting my hand up against the front of the kennel.

Kevin shook his head yes, so I opened the door to go in. Ralphy Bear slowly walked over to me. Leaning down, I took his matted head into my hands. He gazed up at me, looking deep into my eyes with a look of trust. Carefully, I moved my hand over his head and down his back, feeling the tight mats that covered his entire body, clumps and clumps of them. Reaching farther down, I felt the mats on his legs and between his toes.

When I reached back up to his head and touched his ears, he winced in pain. I gently tried to feel around each ear and realized the mats were stuck to the back of his head. I tugged gently on them to see if they would loosen, but he whimpered, and I knew it was painful for him. I knew we needed to get this poor dog help. Leaning back on my heels, I looked over at Kevin.

"This is awful," I moaned.

"Under these conditions, would we have to return this dog to his owner?" Kevin asked.

"Well, I hope not, because this is neglect," I responded.

"I agree," Kevin said, blowing out his breath.

He stuffed his hands deep into his pockets, and I could see the balls of his fists.

"We need to get animal control involved," I stated. "Have you taken good pictures of him?"

"Yes, I took pictures yesterday when he came in and sent them over to the director."

I gave Ralphy Bear a careful pat before I stood to leave. As we walked away, I looked back at the poor, bedraggled dog sitting among his masses of snarled and unkempt hair, determined to get him help.

Our director had called animal control, and she came in later that morning. We directed her to Pod G, where Ralphy Bear was kenneled. This particular animal control officer had a boisterous personality. Passionate in her beliefs, she strongly believed how animals should be cared for. She loved animals and could not hide her feelings when people mistreated them.

She did her job and did it well, not caring if people liked her or not.

When it came to abused animals, she doled out animal cruelty charges and fines. If they argued with her, she had a sharp tongue and used it, backing it up behind her badge. She was gone for a few minutes before we heard her coming back noisily through the dog run doors. They banged loudly against the walls as she angrily lunged toward the front desk, already at full volume.

"Who the HELL owns that poor dog in kennel twenty-six?" she yelled at the top of her lungs.

Our director, overhearing Officer Baily's rampage from her office, came out to calm her down. She knew people were visiting the shelter, intermingling around the front counter or in the hallways, and they could hear Officer Baily's outburst.

"Well, (s#**)," she yelled. "Whoever owns him is not getting him back!"

She stood uncompromisingly in front of us, her arms folded.

"Officer Baily, he's a stray," our director said, trying to calm her down.

Taking her by the arm, she directed her into her office so they could talk. After the door closed behind them, we could still hear Officer Baily's expletives. Left at the front counter, we looked at the astonished faces of the visitors. Heather picked up a packet of papers, waving them in front of them.

"She's very animated," she stated, smiling tranquilly.

They stood wide-eyed, staring at us for a few moments, and then hurried out toward the dog runs, curious about what could have caused such a reaction from the animal control officer.

Later, when Officer Baily was leaving, she gave us strict orders not to return Ralphy Bear to his owners.

"If they come in or call, I want their information. I want to question them about how their dog got into this condition, because they need to understand animal neglect laws in this state."

Personally, I thought I wouldn't want to receive that call from her.

Ralphy Bear remained in our care for the full seventy-two hours. After his hold was up, we called the vet clinic to make an appointment to have him groomed and given a health checkup.

On the fourth day of his stay, a middle-aged couple came in looking for their missing dog. Emmi sent them back to the dog runs to see if the dog was in one of our kennels. When they returned to the front counter, they declared that Ralphy Bear belonged to them. Emmi wrote down their names, phone numbers, and addresses; then she handed them the phone number of animal control.

"You will have to make contact with animal control before you can claim your dog," she informed them.

"What do you mean, call animal control?" the woman said indignantly. "That is our dog, and we want him back, NOW."

She folded her arms in front of her, staring at Emmi and Heather.

"Are you telling me we can't reclaim our dog?" the man asked.

"Yes, that was the directive of our animal control officer," Emmi stated.

Now, the man's face turned red with anger, and he started raising his voice.

"YOU WILL return my dog, and YOU WILL do it NOW."

I heard the yelling from my office and came out to see what was going on. Emotions can run high when it comes to owners and their pets. If staff see someone becoming confrontational at the front desk or anywhere in the building, they must involve our director. She will talk with the person and try to find a solution to de-escalate the situation.

But before we could involve her that morning, she too had already overheard the couple yelling and came out of her office to talk with them.

"Good morning," she said, introducing herself, holding her hand out in a friendly manner. "How can I help you?"

The woman calmed down some but refused to shake her hand. Instead, she pointed her finger at our director, demanding,

"We want our dog back, NOW."

Our director continued to speak in a polite voice.

"Well, your dog came to the shelter in poor condition, so we had to involve animal control. She told us not to return your dog until she speaks with you."

"HOW DARE YOU," the woman yelled. "WE are great dog owners, AND there is nothing wrong with him, OR THE CARE HE HAS."

"Well, we don't agree with you, and neither does animal control," our director continued calmly. "He came into the shelter in poor condition, severely matted. He needs a vet to remove the mats, and we've also found his teeth are in poor condition and will require cleaning and possibly extractions."

Sympathetically, she looked between the two people in front of her.

"I was wondering if there is a problem with money? We have programs available for low-income people who cannot care for their pets and may need assistance."

This seemed to enrage the couple even further, and they continued to argue with her. Heather was standing at the front counter behind them. She waved at me, pointing toward the glass front doors. I looked out to see what she was pointing at and could see Officer Baily turning into the parking lot. She braked her vehicle to a stop next to the new Prius the couple had arrived in.

When she walked into the shelter, the woman noticed her and shook her finger at her.

"I SUPPOSE you are the one WHO HAS PUT A HOLD ON OUR DOG," she yelled.

"Well, I don't know," Officer Baily smiled. "Who is your dog?"

She looked intently at the unhappy couple standing in front of her.

"MAX," they both shouted in unison.

Heather cleared her throat and quietly said, "Ralphy Bear. They are the owners of Ralphy Bear."

"HIS NAME'S NOT RALPHY BEAR," the man yelled. "HIS NAME'S MAX, and YOU need to do YOUR JOB and talk with THESE PEOPLE."

Infuriated, he stepped closer to Officer Baily, getting his face close to hers. Then, lowering his voice, he said,

"They told us they won't return Max to us until we have talked with you, so here we are." He stepped even closer. "LET'S TALK."

Officer Baily's whole countenance immediately changed. She became erect and straightened to her full ex–army drill sergeant height. Puffing out her chest, she stabbed her finger toward the man's chest, bellowing,

"WHAT THE HELL!" she roared. "I SUPPOSE you drove here in that new car sitting in the parking lot, but you CAN'T AFFORD to take care of your DOG. What kind of piece of (s#^!) ARE YOU?"

"HOW DARE YOU!" the woman yelled, sucking in her breath.

"I DO DARE," Officer Baily yelled back. "AND not only am I going to call you names, but I'm giving you a HUGE

FINE FOR ANIMAL NEGLECT!" she emphasized, now poking her finger toward the woman before she continued.

"Are YOU really going to stand there and tell me YOU could not see your dog needed grooming and vet care? It is negligence, and YOU ARE NOT GETTING HIM BACK."

The couple were not ready for this type of response from an animal control officer. But they quickly recovered, and getting their bearings, threatened everyone with a lawsuit.

Officer Baily was used to this kind of threat and continued.

"I'm charging YOU with animal neglect, so YOU CAN TAKE THAT TO COURT, BABY." She stared the couple down. "DO I MAKE MYSELF CLEAR?" she shouted.

The owners recoiled at her bellows and stood open mouthed, staring at her. I thought at any moment she was going to order both of them to the floor for a hundred pushups. She stared the man directly in the eye, unyielding, and did not back away. The man backed up and stepped around her, pulling his wife toward the doors.

"YOU HAVE NOT HEARD THE LAST OF THIS, AND WE ARE CALLING YOUR SUPERVISOR."

"GOOD," Officer Baily shouted. "I AM the supervisor. Call ME any time."

They hurried out of the building and got into their car to leave. We stood looking at one another, waiting for the tension in the air to settle.

"Start taking applications for that poor dog," Officer Baily commanded.

"I will hold him for ten more days and then sign a release for him. I doubt they will be back." She blew out her breath. "Take lots of pictures of him and get him to the vet as soon as you can."

"Do you think they will try to get him back?" Heather asked.

"They're not stupid; they have been neglectful, and they know it. I will leave a message with them later this afternoon and send off a big fine. That should scare the (s#**) out of them. After he has seen the vet, put him on the website and get him adopted."

She blew out her breath again, releasing the pent-up tension.

"That felt good," she blurted out, smiling. "Giving them a piece of my mind made my day, the pieces of CRAP."

She pounded her fist on the countertop.

"The unfortunate thing is," she said, "they will most likely get another dog."

She pounded her fist one last time on the countertop and walked away. The last thing we heard from her was more obscenities as she cursed her way out of the building.

When her taillights flashed red and were out of sight, we stood listening to the quiet of the room. Our director looked around, relieved the confrontation was over, and turned to go back into her office. When she reached the door, she turned back and looked at each of us and said, "I will not have that kind of language from any of my staff members in this shelter."

Heather, who tried to ease the tension that was still permeating the room, stood at attention and saluted her.

"Yes, MA'AM, Director MA'AM," she yelled out.

The following day, Dr. Vincent stopped by the shelter to examine Ralphy Bear. After the examination, he said he would come by the next morning to pick him up and take him to his vet clinic. There, they would shave him and clean his teeth, performing any necessary dental work.

Early the next morning, Dr. Vincent came to pick Ralphy Bear up. Ralphy Bear plodded beside Dr. Vincent, happy to be out of the confines of his kennel. As he walked, the mats swayed back and forth, making him look as if he were carrying another animal on his back.

"Unbelievable," Dr. Vincent said as they walked by.

We waved them off, knowing that when Ralphy Bear returned, he would feel so much better without the tormenting, painful mats pulling on his skin. His teeth would be clean and also free of pain.

We waited in anticipation all afternoon for the metamorphosis of Ralphy Bear, but we were not expecting the transformation that walked through the doors later in the day. We squealed with delight and amazement at the beautiful dog who stood before us.

"Wow!" Emmi said, delighted.

We ran around the counter to greet Ralphy Bear. Kneeling down in front of him, we petted his soft coat. It was a rich brown color, and he still had the cinnamon-colored nose. We could see his ears now, and they were small and round, pricking up with the tips bent down like a Chow's. He greeted each of us, licking our faces.

Ralphy Bear knew someone had liberated him from the misery of knotted mats, which had twisted tightly to his skin and caused him torment and pain whenever he moved. Now he was free, and his freedom allowed him the liberty of movement. With all the surrounding excitement, he zoomed around the room, enjoying his freedom of movement without pain.

"He's a real trooper," Dr. Vincent said, laughing with us.

While we lavished attention on Ralphy Bear, Dr. Vincent went out to his pickup and lifted a large black garbage bag from the back of the truck. When he came back in, he set it down in front of the counter.

"Save that for Officer Baily in case she needs it," Dr. Vincent said, a scowl on his face.

Heather opened it to look inside, and it contained the mats that had been removed from Ralphy Bear.

"Wow," Heather exclaimed.

Reaching down, Dr. Vincent petted Ralphy Bear.

"He is such a friendly dog," he said. "He never fussed while we were handling him."

He reached into his pocket and handed Emmi some antibiotics.

"His teeth were terrible, and we cleaned them," he said. "He had hair wrapped around a lot of them, and it took us a long time to remove it. We also had to extract four of them. Removing the mats took about four hours because my staff was trying to be so careful. We used anesthesia to put him under, but he seems to have recovered well."

He pulled Ralphy Bear into his arms and hugged him.

"You're a good-natured dog," he said, cupping Ralphy Bear's face in his hands. "I hope you find a loving family soon who will love you and treat you well."

We were amazed at the garbage bag full of mats and kept it for Officer Baily as evidence. She came two days later to sign Ralphy Bear's release. She was standing at the front counter talking with staff when a volunteer came around the corner with Ralphy Bear.

Officer Baily acknowledged the volunteer and bent down to pet the dog.

"Who are you?" she said, baby-talking him. "You look like a nice dog."

"That's Ralphy Bear," Emmi said, curious to see her reaction.

Officer Baily stood up, looking at us astonished.

"No ($**)," she swore. "No way."

"Yup," Emmi said, laughing. "They groomed him and cleaned his teeth two days ago," she said.

"Well, I'll be damned," Officer Baily laughed.

She got back down on the floor to admire him. Taking her phone out of her pocket, she started taking pictures, snapping shots from every angle.

Leaning back on her heels, she exclaimed, "I can't believe it, you look like a different dog, and you look so much better."

Reaching down, she folded him into her arms, cuddling him.

"Now, sweetie pie," she cooed. "You need a good home with a special family who will take good care of you."

Ralphy Bear wagged his stub tail as he licked her on the face.

"He knows we rescued him, doesn't he?" Officer Baily said, looking up at us, laughing.

"I love this dog," she declared.

Over the next couple of weeks, Ralphy Bear lived up to his good nature. He was amiable, kind, and caring. He seemed to have a sixth sense about people and knew when they were distressed, hurting, or in pain. Approaching them, he would move close and sit down to lay his head on their lap. Looking up with affection and concern, he would try to comfort them.

To him, it did not matter if they were adults, children, or another animal; his concern was to bring comfort by his closeness. I have observed that dogs rescued from bad situations appreciate the new life they have. They understand compassion, kindness, and love and are grateful to the people who have rescued them.

You may think I am humanizing dogs—not so. By nature, dogs are much kinder, loyal, and unselfish than humans ever could be. Benevolent by nature, they love people, and they only wish to be loved and cared for. I think we could learn a lot from them.

Ralphy Bear, like other rescued dogs who have survived

terrible situations, understands pain, suffering, hunger, meanness, fear, loneliness, unkind words, and abuse, but they still love. I think that because of their deep devotion to mankind; they have become our teachers, showing us how to love, and how I wish humanity would learn from them.

Ralphy Bear had been with us for a month when a woman walked into the shelter looking for a dog. She introduced herself as Marlene and told us she was the administrator at a senior assisted home called Bolton's Manor.

"We have twenty residents in our care who would benefit from having a dog," she said in a sweet southern drawl. "He would become the resident dog, so he or she would need to be a small dog, very affectionate, and well trained."

"I have the perfect dog for you," I said. "His name is Ralphy Bear, but he is not small; he's more of a medium-sized dog."

She shook her head at my suggestion.

"No, no! It needs to be a small dog," she said.

I looked over at the dog board to see if we had any small dogs that would fit her needs, but my eyes kept falling on Ralphy Bear's name. The woman watched me closely while I stared at the board and then asked, "May I have a look around to see if one of your dogs catches my eye?"

"Sure," I told her, feeling disappointed because she would not consider Ralphy Bear.

"If you see someone you like, come back up front, and we will get them out for you."

Watching her walk toward the dog runs, I said to Emmi,

"Ralphy Bear would be perfect."

"I know," she answered back. "But she thinks a small dog would work best for them. Let's see who sparks her interest."

In a few minutes, Marlene was back, wanting to see a little Jack Russell. We got him out for her so she could take him for a walk, but she soon returned, stating he barked the whole time.

Next, she picked a toy poodle, but he marked everything outdoors and in. Pops the pug was too old, and Muffin, the Bichon, ignored her and was aloof. After meeting all the small dogs she thought were appropriate, she felt disheartened and overwhelmed.

"I know you are tired, but would you please take a peek at Ralphy Bear?" I again suggested.

"You can sit down in the office, and I will bring him in for you to meet."

"Well, all right," she said, sounding unconvinced. "My mother always said, Never leave a stone unturned."

I took her to an office and excitedly ran back to the kennels to get Ralphy Bear out. When I brought him into the office, I could tell she did not approve, but she was a good sport about it and called him over to her. Shutting the door, I left so they could get acquainted.

The office had a window in it, and Emmi and I stood behind the front counter watching them. Ralphy Bear walked over to her and gently laid his head on her lap. Looking up, he searched her face with his soft brown liquid eyes.

"You're very soft," we could hear her say as she petted him. "What a gentleman you are."

We left them for about ten minutes before Emmi went to see how they were getting on.

Marlene smiled. "He seems to be a very nice dog."

"He is," Emmi said. "He is very easy to walk, never jumps on anyone, does not bark, and has never marked on anything. He adores people and gives everyone his full attention."

She briefed Marlene on Ralphy Bear's history and the circumstances of how he came to the shelter.

"Well, you sound just perfect," she said, holding his head in her hands. "I wish you were smaller, though."

"We think he is perfect," Emmi stated emphatically. "And I

think he would love living at your facility where he could comfort your residents. He would love to have a vocation where he could devote his life to people, bringing joy and comfort to people."

Marlene still held Ralphy Bear's head in her hands while looking deep into his eyes.

"Well, he is much larger than I had in mind, but I am interested in him. Could I bring a couple of the residents to meet him tomorrow?" she asked. "I need to see how he responds to them."

"Absolutely," Emmi replied.

Emmi made the appointment for the next day, and everyone thought Marlene would cancel, but we were wrong. She came the following afternoon with two of her senior residents. We put them into an office, and I went to get Ralphy Bear.

When I walked in with him, he greeted Marlene, and noticing the man, he sat down next to him, placing his head in his lap. Soon he noticed the woman and walked over to her, gently laying his head on her lap. Her arthritic hands tenderly moved down his head and over his back, stroking him.

The man asked if they could take him for a walk, so we harnessed Ralphy Bear and handed the leash to Marlene. They walked slowly down the sidewalk, with Ralphy Bear walking beside them. He did not seem disturbed by the cane or wheelchair but kept pace, matching their steps.

When they returned, we could hear their lively chatter and noticed cheerful smiles on their faces. Marlene had the brightest smile and announced with excitement,

"He is perfect," she laughed. "And we were wondering if we could do the adoption today, so he could go home with us."

Emmi took them into the adoption room to complete

Ralphy Bear's adoption, making him the newest resident of Bolton's Manor.

Every once in a while, we wondered how Ralphy Bear was doing. We knew he had found a wonderful home and was very busy watching over and caring for its twenty residents.

It was a full year before we heard from anyone. The fall days were cooling, and the leaves on the trees were turning beautiful hues of yellow, orange, and red when one day a big package and letter arrived from Bolton's Manor. Our director gathered the staff and opened the letter to read it to us.

Dear Shelter Staff,

I just have to tell you how well Ralphy is doing. He settled in, making friends with every resident and staff member here at Bolton's Manor. We shortened his name to Ralphy because it is easier for the residents to remember and say. He adjusted immediately, loving each person and responding to their individual needs. He has become the official doorgreeter and welcomes visitors who come to visit their loved ones. He also greets the staff each day and the vendors who deliver goods to our facility. He greets each resident in the morning, and he says goodnight to them as they get ready for bed. If a person is not feeling well, he lays by their feet or near their bed, attempting to reassure them with his presence. The ambulant residents take him for walks several times a day, or he will go to the patio with the few who have a harder time walking. On the patio, he sits or lies near them in the warm sunshine.

He had been with us for about a month when, in the middle of the night, we found him barking outside a man's door. Ralphy never barks, so we knew something was wrong. When we checked, we found the man on the floor. He was having a heart attack, and because Ralphy alerted us to the man's emergency, we were able to help him. This has happened a couple of times when one of our residents is sick or in distress. So Ralphy has become a talked-about hero around here.

We also have a resident named Eleanor, who was cranky and unhappy with everyone. She seemed determined not to like it here, finding fault with everything. When Ralphy came, she did not like him. Shooing him away, she called him a dirty dog and was constantly complaining about him. With his kind personality, he made it his goal to win her heart. He followed her around or lay a short distance away with his head down on his front paws, watching her.

This went on for a couple of weeks with Ralphy keeping a safe distance. Soon we found him lying outside her room while she napped. One day while sitting in the dayroom reading, Eleanor dropped her glasses on the floor. She has severe arthritis, which makes it hard for her to grasp and pick things up. So while she was bent over trying to reach them, Ralphy watched her struggling. He stood up and trotted over to where her glasses were lying. Gently, he picked them up and placed them on her lap. She sat quietly, looking down at her glasses and then looked over at Ralphy and smiled.

Reaching out, she gave him a pat on the head, praising him. He had won her heart, and she is now one of his devoted admirers, bragging to all visitors about what a smart dog he is.

Ralphy has become a beloved member of our community. He makes each person, staff member, or visitor feel special, needed, valued, and loved. If someone leaves us, he comforts us while he also grieves.

We have given him a birthday of September 17, the day we adopted him. We celebrated with a big party, serving cake and ice cream, with Ralphy receiving gifts.

Because Ralphy is so loved here, he has no need for anything, so we will send these gifts to you to use for the dogs who are waiting for homes. We end the party with stories of how much Ralphy means to each person. I do not know how we lived without him. Every day is a blessing and a gift with his presence.

Thank you for rescuing Ralphy Bear and giving him a second chance at life. Thank you for being persistent about introducing him to us and bringing him into the life of our community. We can't express how much we love him and the joy he brings.

Sincerely,

Marlene, the residents, and staff at Bolton's Manor.

P.S. That is Eleanor sitting next to Ralphy with her hand on his head.

Inside the letter was a picture of twenty smiling residents and their staff members, with Ralphy Bear sitting in front of them. Each resident held a balloon with Ralphy's name on it, and Ralphy was wearing a party hat.

A dog will teach you unconditional love. If you can have that, things won't be too bad.

ROBERT WAGNER

LOLA AND LOUI

WHEN I CAME into the shelter one cool and frosty morning, Heather was standing behind the front desk surrounded by staff members. Curious, I walked up behind them to look over Heather's shoulder to see what she was holding. In her arms was a Chihuahua. Her coat was a lovely dark grey with a white patch under her chin and down her belly. She had white socks on all four feet, and she pushed her pricked ears forward, listening to all the ladies murmuring to her sympathetically.

Heather noticed me standing there and held the little dog up to show me it's bulging belly. Now I understood why all the staff were feeling sorry for her, because her pregnant belly was grotesquely huge.

"That has to be uncomfortable," I said, staring at the veins that ran along the stretched skin.

"I know, poor thing," Heather said, trying to maneuver the little dog into a more comfortable position.

"How many puppies do you think are in there?" she asked.

"A lot," I responded.

A few minutes later, Emmi walked in, and Heather turned to show her the pregnant Chihuahua.

"Oh, wow!" Emmi said. "Can she even walk?"

"Barely," Heather frowned. "It might be easier for her to roll."

Emmi reached out to pet the dog, and Heather asked her the same question she had asked me.

"How many puppies do you think she has in there?"

"Quite a few," Emmi stated, concerned. "Or maybe one big puppy."

We had not thought of that, and our worry for the little dog increased. Now we were apprehensive and wondered if she could deliver an oversized puppy.

"She must be due anytime, so we need to get her to Dr. Vincent and see how many puppies are in there," Emmi said. "And we also need to find a foster for her who can closely monitor her."

"I'll call Dr. Vincent this morning," Heather replied, handing the dog over to me to hold.

Even though I was trying to be careful, she grunted uncomfortably while I held her.

"Does she have a name?" I asked. "And where did she come from?"

"Her name's Lola," Heather answered. "A lady brought her in last evening before we closed. She told us she thought the dog needed to see a vet, and she didn't have the money to cover a vet bill. We were suspicious that she is a breeder, so of course we took the dog from her."

"Well," Pat huffed. "If people spayed and neutered their animals instead of breeding them to sell puppies, they could prevent all this."

We all agreed, but our concern at the moment was for this sweet little dog in my arms.

"She seems very sweet and gentle with all these strangers staring at her," I stated.

"You are sweet, aren't you, honey," Heather said, reaching out to take her from me. "I was afraid to leave her here alone last night, so I took her home with me. She was very sweet to my daughter and good with all my dogs."

"Maybe you should foster her?" I suggested.

Heather shook her head. "If I took her, I wouldn't get any sleep. I would check on her all night, worried she was going into labor."

"Just a suggestion, no pressure," I said, smiling.

Even though Heather had firmly stated she was not taking her home, I knew when evening came she would look for a carrier and stuffing it with a nice, comfy blanket so she could take Lola home. In fact, Lola would most likely stay with Heather for the rest of her pregnancy and puppy-raising. Heather had fostered many puppies for the shelter throughout the years. She had a sling she would throw over her shoulders to carry orphaned puppies or kittens in. Nestled inside, they contentedly slept, cozy and warm. I knew she would never consider leaving Lola's care with another foster, even if it caused her insomnia.

Later in the morning, Heather took Lola to the vet clinic to see Dr. Vincent. After returning to the shelter, we gathered around her to hear what Dr. Vincent had discovered.

"He took an X-ray, which shows one large puppy," Heather told us. "He's advising us to give the puppy one more week, and then he will do a caesarean section."

Heather gently rubbed Lola's pricked ears with her fingers before continuing.

"Dr. Vincent said if Lola goes into labor or is in any kind of distress, he will do the C-section sooner."

"We'd better start calling some of our fosters to see if they can take her," Emmi said.

"I've decided to take her," Heather told us, waving us away. "Dr. Vincent gave me his cell phone number and told me to call him day or night if Lola needs him."

With a determined look on her face, she picked up Lola's carrier to take her into the adoption room. In a quiet corner of the room, she laid a nice soft bed and covered it with an extra soft blanket. She let Lola out of the carrier and placed her in the middle of the bed, tucking her in. For the rest of the day, Heather checked on her frequently, and so did the rest of the staff. Anticipating labor, we were now on baby watch.

I don't know which endorphins a woman's brain releases to spark sympathy for a pregnant animal, but we all felt a need to cuddle and reassure Lola. Perhaps it was because most of us had had children, which caused us to feel empathy and a need to comfort her.

When evening came, and it was time to close the shelter, Heather took Lola home. Each morning in the coming days, she would bring Lola back to work with her so she could closely watch her. By the third day, we could see exhaustion on Heather's face and knew she was not sleeping well. Talking among ourselves, we wondered if she could hold out much longer.

"I can't sleep," she complained one morning. "I'm getting up every hour to check on her. If I hear her grunt, groan, or sigh, I shoot out of my bed thinking she has gone into labor."

Concerned for her, Emmi suggested, "Maybe you better let one of us take her for the next couple of nights."

Heather would not even consider Emmi's suggestion and shook her head.

"I'll be fine," she said in a weary voice. "I'm just a little tired and ready for this puppy to arrive."

The next morning, Heather texted Emmi to say she was at the vet clinic with Lola, and Dr. Vincent was preparing her for surgery. Like a nervous family waiting in the waiting room, we spent the rest of the morning expecting a call back from Heather. At 11:00, she walked into the shelter ready to show us pictures of the new puppy.

"Isn't he cute?" She murmured, like an adoring grandmother.

She held her phone up so everyone could see the pictures. We all leaned in to look, and we were amazed at his size.

"What the heck," Pat stated bluntly. "I can't believe how big he is."

"Dr. Vincent said Lola did great and will make a full recovery," Heather said, still looking down at her phone.

"How much did he weigh?" I asked.

"Oh!" she said, looking at me surprised. "I forgot to ask, but Dr. Vincent said Lola wouldn't have been able to deliver him naturally."

We looked again at the picture. The puppy didn't look like a Chihuahua at all. Heather was holding him, and he filled up her hand. He had a very round head with a smushed-up nose. His hair was white with brown patches, and each eye had a brown patch over it which ran down his ears. His ears were on the sides of his head and flopped down.

"Do you think the dad was a pug?" Emmi asked.

"Who knows," Heather answered back. "I'm just glad he has arrived, and he's healthy."

She held up the phone again so we could see another picture.

"Isn't he cute?" she cooed. "Oh, look at this one."

In this picture, he was lying next to his mother.

"Wow," we all said in unison.

"Is it possible his father was a Golden Retriever?" Pat said jokingly.

"Noooo!" we all replied simultaneously, staring in wonderment at the picture in front of us.

Lola and her puppy stayed with Heather for the next six weeks. When she brought them back to the shelter, we tucked them into the employees' bathroom out of the public eye. We all talked about the dad, trying to guess what his lineage was, and of course, it was not a Golden Retriever.

We were certain he might have been a Cavalier King Charles Spaniel. The puppy had medium-long white hair with patches of brown. The brown circled each eye, and they were a deep brown, round and prominent. His black nose was short and upturned. We all would sneak into the bathroom to play with him, and it wasn't long before we were calling him Loui. Entering the bathroom, we would adoringly call his name, and he would yip with joy as he bounced on his front feet toward us. Lola was very attentive and proud of her boy. He had passed her up, but she still did her job correcting any bad manners and teaching him good dog skills. The staff was in love with Loui and happily spoiled him. We also loved Lola, with her gentle, charismatic and sweet nature. She loved everyone, alluring them into her kind, peaceful world, but one thing she absolutely would not tolerate was the shelter cat named Princess. If Princess walked too close to the bathroom door, Lola would erupt with high-pitched barking. Protecting her oversized puppy, she was having no foolishness from the lower-class cat.

When Loui was eight weeks old, we moved them together into the small dog area. The visitors who came to the shelter were surprised to read that Lola and Loui were mother and son. Some people thought we were joking and questioned us.

Composed and straight-faced, we assured them that the two dogs were really mother and son.

At eight weeks, Lola had weaned Loui, and they were ready to go to their homes. We posted their pictures on the website and started taking applications for them. Over the next week, many people applied, and there was a lot of excitement, especially with Loui. We were ready to choose homes for them when the woman who had brought Lola in came back to the shelter. Taking Emmi aside, she informed her she wanted Lola and Loui back. Shocked at her request, Emmi took her into an office to talk with her.

"When you brought Lola to the Humane Society, you signed a surrender form releasing her into our care," she explained to her.

"I didn't release her," the woman stated. "I brought her here because I couldn't afford the vet care Lola was going to need."

Emmi was astonished this woman believed she could drop off a dog, never call to see how she was, and then come back months later and try to reclaim her.

"We have applications on both of them, and are going to adopt them out," Emmi informed her.

The woman leaned forward in her chair, looking at Emmi intently.

"They are my dogs!" she insisted. "I want you to return them to me now, or I'm calling my lawyer."

Emmi picked up the phone to call our director, asking her to come into her office. After she stepped into the room, the woman realized she was now talking with the director. She became more belligerent, informing her that she wanted her dogs returned. Our director tried reasoning with her, but the woman became more hostile.

"I will sue you, I will," she yelled. "You have no right to keep my dogs from me."

After a few more minutes of trying to talk, our director leaned back in her chair to wait for the woman to calm down.

"You're absolutely right," our director said in a soothing voice. "I have decided to let you take them back. We will have all their paperwork ready for you tomorrow, but because they are in our system, we will have to adopt them back to you, and there will be a fee."

"That's fine," the woman bluntly stated. "I can afford that."

Emmi could not believe her ears and tried to interject, but our director held up her hand, warning her to remain quiet.

"So are we in agreement?" Our director said, still trying to placate the woman.

"Yes, I'll be here first thing tomorrow," the woman said.

Satisfied because she had got her way, the woman agreed to return on the following day to complete the adoptions. Happily, she waved goodbye and strutted out the shelter doors. Once we heard what had happened, we were shocked and angry, incredulous with our director at what she had agreed to do. We crowded behind the front desk in disbelief, staring disapprovingly at her. When she walked out of the office, she picked up some papers from the top of the counter. Smiling, she looked up at each of us.

"Trust me in this," she said, waving the papers.

We felt enraged. How could she ever think of releasing Lola and Loui back to this woman, who most likely was a breeder?

Again, she smiled. "Trust me."

We all hoped the woman would change her mind and not return to do the adoptions. But the next day right at 11:00, she stepped through the Humane Society doors. Disapprovingly, Pat ushered her into the adoption room and informed her that our director would be in shortly to do the adoptions. Twenty minutes later, both our director and Emmi crossed the hall to enter the office where the woman sat fidgeting.

"Do you want the door shut?" Emmi asked.

"No," our director stated, looking at the staff grouped behind the front counter. "That won't be necessary."

We had gathered behind the front desk so we could overhear what was being said in the office. We were still in disbelief and angry with our director because of her agreement to return Lola and Loui. After they entered the office, our director cordially greeted the woman and took a seat behind the desk opposite her.

"Good afternoon, Mrs. S," she said, holding out her hand to shake hers.

"You remember Emmi?" she asked. "She will help me do Lola's adoption."

The woman looked closely at her.

"I want Loui too," she said, looking between Emmi and our director suspiciously.

"Of course," our director smiled. "We have prepared both adoptions for you."

"I hope you did not spay Lola, because she is one of my best breeder dogs," the woman implied.

Our suspicions were now confirmed, with the woman now acknowledging she was breeding dogs.

"Well, we don't adopt any animals out without their being spayed or neutered," our director answered back. "So, of course, they have both been altered."

"You should have asked my permission before spaying and neutering my dogs," the woman replied, raising her voice.

Listening to the conversation going on in the office, I was amazed at how patient our director was being.

"When you brought Lola to the shelter, you surrendered

her to us because you didn't feel you could afford the veterinarian bills, is that correct?" our director inquired in a casual voice.

"I didn't surrender her," the woman said condescendingly. "She needed vet care, and I didn't have the means to provide that."

"Oh!" our director said pleasantly. "But we have no record of you ever calling to check up on her until now. We assumed Lola was abandoned because you didn't call.

She smiled at the woman before proceeding.

"Under Washington State law, any dog not claimed by an owner within 72 hours becomes the Humane Society's property."

Our director was quiet for a few minutes and then leaned forward in her chair.

"So, Mrs. S, because you legally don't have any claim on them, I feel we are being very kind to you in returning Lola and her puppy," she said firmly.

"Well, I guess you are," the woman grumbled.

"So let's get started," our director said.

Opening a file, she pulled out all the official documents and set them down in front of her. Lifting the top page, she handed it across the desk toward Mrs. S.

"This first page is a bill with the costs incurred to the Humane Society for both dogs. I think you must agree we will have to have compensation for everything we have accumulated for the care of your two dogs."

The woman reached for the paper before responding.

"Well, they are my dogs, so I guess I can recover the money with the sale of the puppy."

The woman took her glasses from her purse and put them on. As she read the charges on the bill, her face blanched, and her mouth tightened into pencil-thin lines in astonishment.

Surrender fee 35.00

Foster care first week 70.00

Veterinarian cost 550.00

Medicine 75.23

Foster care, six weeks 420.00

Spay of Lola 300.00

Rabies, Lola 50.00

Vaccinations, Lola 30.00

Microchip & registration, Lola 75.00

Neuter of Loui 150.00

Two rounds of vaccinations, Loui 60.00

Microchip & registration, Loui 75.00

Adoption fee, Lola, 350.00

Adoption fee, Loui 400.00

Total $2,640.23

She threw the paper across the desk toward our director.

"I can't afford that," she yelled. "You are trying to rob me."

"Mrs. S," our director said, looking at her patiently. "After getting the numbers from our bookkeeper, these are the expenses of Lola and Loui's care. Being a nonprofit, we cannot afford to absorb these costs. Remember, you told us you will pay the fee."

"Well, not $2,640.00." she squeaked out. "I was thinking more like $200.00."

Our director picked up the bill and turned it so the woman could see it. Pointing at the total with her pen, she said,

"You must understand by looking at this bill, the shelter cannot cover the cost for the care of Lola and Loui, even if someone else adopts them."

Emmi cleared her throat. "I'm sorry to interrupt you, but you have forgotten to add the additional charges of boarding fees, which is another $200.00 apiece for both dogs. With the two weeks they spent in our care here at the shelter, it makes the total $3,040.23."

"Oh, my goodness!" our director said, lifting her eyebrows. "You're right!"

She laid the bill back down on the desktop and wrote an additional $400.00 under the total. The woman's face was livid and had turned from red to a grayish blue. She slowly stood up, but before she could speak, our director held up her hands.

"Mrs. S," she said. "We realize this is a lot of money, so why don't you go home and think about it. You can call us back tomorrow or later today and tell us if you want to go through with the adoption."

"There is nothing to think about," the woman said, her voice tight with anger. "I can't afford those fees."

Grabbing the papers off the desk, she yelled, "You are all a bunch of thieves."

Turning, she stomped towards the front doors. When she reached the doors, she turned and waved the papers at the office where our director and Emmi sat.

"Keep her," she shouted. "Keep both of them; they are no good to me anyway because you had them spayed and neutered."

Tearing up the papers, she threw the torn pieces in the air, then, shaking her fist at us, she yelled one last time.

"I'm donating them to you; do whatever you want with them."

Shoving the doors open, she stormed toward her car. Our director sat smiling for a moment before coming out of the office. The satisfied look on her face was gratifying to see, and we started clapping.

"Well done," I said, laughing. "Brilliant."

She smiled and took a long, deep bow and pointed towards

her fellow conspirator. Laughing, Emmi also took a deep bow, waving her hand in front of her, accepting our praise and adulation for her performance.

"I told you to trust me," our director said, with a glint in her eye. "I have been doing this a very long time, and I think I know what I am doing by now."

We happily spent the next few days going through applications, searching for new homes for Lola and Loui. There were so many wonderful applications, and we were having a hard time deciding. Finally, Pat held up an application with a letter attached.

"This one sounds interesting and may give us an answer for both dogs," she said.

She handed the letter across the desk to our director. Unfolding the letter, our director began reading it out loud.

Dear Shelter Staff,

I am writing to you because I'm interested in adopting Loui. I am a retired nurse, and although retired, I am a very active person. I go dancing twice a week, do yoga one day a week, and until recently walked every day. I lost my beloved King Charles last fall, and with his loss, it has taken the joy out of my daily walks. My dog was such a big part of my life, and because I am so lonely, I realize how much I need a new dog to love and share my life with.

Most of the residents in my apartment complex are seniors. The apartment dwellers here are a family and share our lives together. We have many activities, which include potlucks, dances, card playing, and many, many more. We all share a love of animals, and the apartment complex allows people to have pets. If one of the residents is ill, traveling, or needs to get away for the day, we all chip in to help in the care of each other's pets.

I realize you probably have many applications for Loui from others who could love and adore him as much as I would. So that is why I am writing, so you could get to know me a little better. Now that I have shared my request for Loui, I have another request of you. If you search through the applications, there will be another application from my neighbor, Carol Bennet. She put in an application for Lola. She is a retired social worker, and we have been friends for years. She lives in the apartment next to me and lost her dog two years ago. When she lost her beloved Cindy, she had decided not to replace her. After seeing Lola on your website, she thought it would be a wonderful idea to adopt her. If we are both chosen, Lola and Loui could remain right next door to one another. We think it would be an ideal situation for both dogs, and as two active seniors in our 70s, it would bond our friendship even more. We have a lot of life to live and would love to share our love and lives with these two sweet dogs. Would you ever consider that? We both hope so and await your reply.

Sincerely,

Beth Jones.

We sat back in our chairs, knowing this was a perfect solution for Lola and Loui.

"This is perfect," I said.

"I think so too," Emmi agreed, digging for the other application.

Our director sat in thought, thumping the table with her red pen. When Emmi found Carol Bennet's application, she handed it over to the director. Because of Beth's wonderful letter and the fact that Lola and Loui would live close to one another, it was a simple choice. Our director wrote "approved" on both applications and handed them back to Emmi. Pulling her glasses off, she laid them on her desktop. With a big smile, she pointed the pen at Emmi and said,

"Call them and see if they can come in today to do the adoptions."

Early in the afternoon, Beth and her neighbor Carol came to the shelter to complete the adoptions. Because of all that had happened, the staff gave a sigh of relief and were ecstatic that Lola and Loui would remain close to one another. Living next door to each other, they would go on daily walks and be able to interact often. Now the two ladies would have the fun of telling people that Lola and Loui were mother and son.

When the Christmas season rolled around, we received a card with two smiling ladies, each holding their dog. Both dogs were dressed in red sweaters. Loui's had a doggy Rudolph with a red nose on his, and Lola's had a white ruffle. We stood looking over our director's shoulder at the picture.

"Aren't they adorable?" Heather stated proudly.

"And look how happy they all are," I added.

"We really rescued them from a bad situation," Pat added.

"That was an impressive performance, wasn't it?" our director replied, looking at Emmi.

"A theatrical genius," Emmi answered back.

"Yup, we set the stage, and she performed the drama," our director laughed.

By now we were all laughing, glad to have the melodrama over and the main characters safely placed in their forever homes.

"Sometimes you have to do whatever it takes to rescue an animal," our director said, laughing louder.

Emmi and our director did not receive an Emmy for their performance that day, but they should have. Our Emmy was the rescue of two wonderful dogs, which was the best reward and honor anyone could have ever received.

It is amazing how much love and laughter dogs bring into our lives and even how much closer we become with each other because of them.

JOHN GROGAN

ROSCO

"What a strange-looking little man," Pat said.

I followed her gaze down the hall to see a man in a brown suit, which hung limply on his slight frame. His feet looked way too big for him as he trudged down the hallway with a gimpy limp. Later, as I walked past the small dog area, I could see the man waving at me as he tried to get my attention.

"Excuse me," he uttered in a wispy, low voice, which was hard to hear. "I am curious about that impressive, diminutive dog barking at me."

I looked into the kennel he was pointing at. Rosco, a small black and brown Dachshund, stood there barking.

"Oh!" I answered. "That is Rosco."

Looking closer through the kennel glass at Rosco, the man pushed his glasses further up his nose before replying.

"He is an extraordinary-looking dog, and has a very stentorian voice, quite loud."

The man turned, looking directly at me from behind his thick glasses, which made his eyes look huge through the opaque lenses.

"Oh, I'm sorry," he said, holding out his hand. "Forgive me for being so rude. My name is Oliver Welder."

As I took his hand, I thought, *Where have I heard that name before?*

"You weren't rude, Mr. Welder," I said. "My name is Julie."

"Now that we have introduced ourselves, tell me about this elfin fellow," he said. "I can tell he is quite puckish."

I looked over at Rosco and then, turning my gaze back at the curious man standing in front of me, I replied.

"Mr. Welder, Rosco is all of what you have observed, but I must tell you he is also blind."

He looked closer at Rosco before responding.

"We all have our frailties; some are quite noticeable, and others are hidden within."

Sometimes, disabled dogs and cats came to the shelter. Some had hearing problems, and may have been deaf. Some had missing limbs, and some were blind, as Rosco was. He came to us through animal control at the end of a hot summer day.

Earlier in the afternoon, the clouds had thickened and turned dark. Soon there was lightning, with the loud booming of thunder. A gentle rain followed, creating a hazy mist as it evaporated off the hot pavement. Loud noises frighten some dogs, and we thought Rosco might have been one of them. Fearful, he must have panicked, and then ran to get away from the booming. We posted him on our website hoping his owner would come to claim him, but after two weeks we knew they were not coming. This surprised us because this breed is such a popular breed. When they come into the shelter, they will have a brief stay before being adopted out.

After animal control released him, I pulled him into my office to do an evaluation on him. I took him outdoors for a walk and noticed he startled easily. Inside the play yard, he dove into the tall grass to smell and snoop around. I watched the grass sway and tilt forward as he plowed his way through it. When his nose was satisfied, he sat down and started crying. I waded through the grass to pick him up.

Laughing, I scolded him. "You're supposed to be a hunting dog, and you can't find your way out of tall grass."

Kevin walked up to the fence and leaned against it.

"Why is he doing that?" he asked.

"What?" I replied, looking down at Rosco.

"That!" he said, pointing.

Watching Rosco, I could see what Kevin was talking about. Rosco was high-stepping on his sturdy little legs with his nose high in the air, as if to get a scent. As he moved forward, he bumped into the fence.

"Oh, oh," I said. "Do you think he's blind?"

Kevin looked at me surprised. "I wonder! Yesterday when I reached down to pick him up I startled him, and he tried to nip me."

I walked over to Rosco, calling his name. Turning, he came towards me. Leaning down, I carefully touched him before picking him up. Looking into his eyes, I could see they were a clear brown and not cloudy. Placing him back on the ground, I watched to see what he would do. As he walked away from me, I took my scarf off, dropping it in front of him. He did not stop to walk around it, or jump over it, but walked right into it.

I put his leash back on him so we could walk around the play yard. I was not careful of what was lying in front of him as we walked, and every time he bumped into, or stumbled over them.

"I don't think he's seeing," I said, looking at Kevin sadly.

I picked Rosco up to take him back indoors. Some of the staff were busy at the front desk as we approached.

"I think Rosco's blind," I told them.

Both Emmi and Pat leaned forward to look into Rosco's eyes.

"Why do you think that?" Emmi asked.

"I don't think he's blind," Pat said, unconvinced.

"He is. Watch." I put Rosco down on the floor and walked him towards a wall until he blindly walked into it.

When our director was told, she made an appointment at the vet clinic with Dr. Vincent. We dropped him off the next morning, and later in the afternoon Dr. Vincent brought him back to the shelter.

"Rosco has progressive retinal atrophy," he said, "and yes, he is blind. Unfortunately, there isn't a cure, but Rosco can still live a long, happy life. He will just need a special home."

Now that we had a diagnosis, we were looking for a specific home with people who would keep Rosco safe. Rosco was used to his blindness, and with the resilient personality of the Dachshund breed, he soon won our hearts. Because he was blind, the staff became protective parents to him. I bought a book on blind dogs so I could educate myself and share with the staff what I had learned.

We were his eyes, which made us more careful of his surroundings. To avoid startling him, we learned to call his name as we approached. We also had learned how frightened he was around other dogs, probably because he could not see what their intentions were, and had to depend on his sense of hearing and smell.

If he found himself lost, he would sit and cry, knowing we would run to his rescue. All this made us reluctant to send him outdoors with a stranger who might not be as attentive as we were.

Once we placed him on the website, applications started pouring in. People have enormous hearts and are kind to animals with disabilities. They were not afraid to adopt them, hoping to make their lives better. In Rosco's case, his new owner would need to educate themselves on living with a blind dog. Rosco would be completely reliant on them to keep him out of harm's way.

As each application came in, we went over them, checking to see if they were a good fit for Rosco, but something was always wrong. They may not have had a fenced yard, or they may have had homes with stairs, which would make it hard for Rosco to negotiate safely. We were mainly disappointed that they had neglected to educate themselves about living with a blind dog. Everything had to fall perfectly into place before we could send Rosco into his new home.

Mr. Welder had put an application in for Rosco and was coming to the shelter several days in a row to visit with him. He seemed reserved at first, avoiding a lot of conversation. When forced to communicate with us, he had a very large vocabulary, which sent our brains into tailspins as we tried to comprehend what he was saying.

After a couple of weeks, he began to relax, peppering us with word descriptions, such as:

"Rosco's a charming fellow, and may beguile the birds out of the trees as they are singing classical sonnets over our heads."

The next day he described Rosco's play as:

"He's a talisman, casting a spell of delight and enchantment upon me. It is as if he is sending out puffs of happiness for me to inhale."

His description of his house was:

"It is not much, just a little brown box nestled in the comforts of the woods, but it is sufficient. I am warmed each evening by the coziness of a warm fire in the fireplace. There I rest by the hearth and read."

I looked forward each day when Mr. Welder would visit the shelter to see Rosco. Coming early in the morning, he waited patiently outdoors while smoking his pipe. At eleven, when the doors opened, he carefully tapped the remaining tobacco out of his pipe and placed it neatly into his coat pocket. Fussing with his bow tie to make sure it was neat and tidy, he then straightened his jacket one last time before coming inside. Acknowledging us with a shy greeting, he walked with purpose toward the small dog runs to see Rosco.

"I think that man is weird," Pat said, watching him.

"Oh, I don't think so; he's just very eccentric," I said.

One day when he came inside, he politely approached the front counter to inquire about his application. We too were wondering if our director was going to approve it and allow Mr. Welder to adopt Rosco.

"We haven't heard any news yet," Emmi responded to him.

"Well, I am a very patient man, and I am certain she is a very busy person. Is there an unspecified reason that may be holding up the process?" he inquired.

"I don't know, but I will try to find out," Emmi said, feeling sorry for him.

"Thank you," he smiled. "Meanwhile, it gives me more time to become acquainted with Rosco, and also educate myself on blind dogs."

The following day, he came in with little bells fastened to his shoes. Pat rolled her eyes and gave a disapproving look as he jingled down the hall.

"He is getting weirder by the moment," she quietly blurted out.

"No, he's not," I said, defending him. "I know he's reading the book I gave him about blind dogs. It says if you put bells on your shoes, the dog will know where you are and be able to find you."

Pat huffed as she listened to the bells tinkling down the hall on Mr. Welder's shoes, but I was impressed, and smiled.

A couple of nights later, I woke from a deep sleep and sat straight up in bed. It finally came to me where I had heard the name Oliver Welder.

"Mark, wake up," I said, excitedly shaking him.

"What," he said, annoyed at being woken from a deep slumber.

"Oliver Welder," I said excitedly. "I remember now who he is."

"Uh huh," he said, drowsily yawning.

"He's a famous author," I told him. "He has written many famous books."

"Okay, that's nice; tell me all about it in the morning."

Rolling over, he pulled the blankets over his head.

"No wonder," I said.

Wide awake, I jumped out of bed and ran to my bookcase, pulling books out. Standing there in the dim lamplight, I read the titles of his books. Opening one, it started with the words, *Once when I was a small boy transcending between nine to ten, I woke in the early morning to be greeted by my plump proportioned uncle, saying, 'Come my boy, daybreak will soon dawn upon us. We must be out on the lake before the fish find out we have arrived, and flee to hide from us.'*

I closed the book, slipping it back between two other books. I had heard many stories of the reclusive Mr. Welder, who lived somewhere in the Northwest. They said he stopped attending book signings and declined to speak at lectures when invited. He had been a professor and a brilliant orator, teaching and lecturing on literature. He was a genius with the classics, bringing them to life for his captivated audience. Once the lecture was over, he would separate from the crowd and disappear.

Now, this very famous author was at our shelter trying to adopt Rosco. Even though he seemed odd and hermitlike, I was now on a mission to convince my director to approve his application.

I laid awake the rest of the night making plans, but before I could talk with her the next morning, Mr. Welder jingled into the shelter requesting an interview.

"May I speak with the director?" He asked Emmi respectfully.

"Of course," she said.

Knocking on the director's door, she led him into her office. He introduced himself, holding out his hand to shake hers. She could see he was nervous and invited him to sit down. Sitting down, he eloquently made his case on his desire to adopt Rosco.

"I lived alone for many years before I received my first dog," he said. "He was a sturdy, tough Scottish Terrier, and he filled my home with camaraderie and fellowship. If I had to go somewhere to lecture, I had the reassurance of Scottie's calm presence waiting for me when I returned.

You see, I suffer from great anxiety, and after being in a social setting with so many people, I suffer with disquietude, and my nerves seem fractured. Scottie was such a good friend to me, and upon my return from one of those events we would walk together in the woods until I could recover and regain my composure.

"I no longer have speaking engagements, and now spend my days in the comfort of my home. I loved my little Scottie dog, who recently passed away, leaving me completely alone. I have all the money one needs to care for a dog, and I have read the book your evaluator gave me about blind dogs, plus two others. After reading them, I employed a neighbor who is a handyman to come to my home and do any repairs needed to protect Rosco from any mishap or misadventure that a blind dog could have."

He reached into his coat pocket, pulling out pictures of his home, handing them across the desk toward our director. He showed all the completed work, both inside and outside.

"If I can direct you to the picture of the deck," he said. "You will notice the latticework fence that my neighbor put around the exterior of the deck, making it secure. There is no way of escape, or worry of Rosco ever falling off the deck. So, as you can see, I have done my required homework to prepare for the event of Rosco coming home with me."

Mr. Welder sat back exhausted in the chair. Folding his hands in front of him, he waited for our director's response.

"Mr. Welder," she said, smiling. "I am impressed with how seriously and thoughtfully you have prepared your home for Rosco, and I think we could never find a better home for him than yours."

She looked across her desk at Mr. Welder. "So yes, I will approve your application."

She searched through the application files on Rosco, and when she came across Mr. Welder's, she wrote *approved.* Looking back up, she could see big tears rolling down Mr. Welder's cheeks, dropping onto the lapel of his worn tweed jacket.

"Would you like to do the adoption today?" She asked, handing him a tissue.

"Yes, I would love to," he said, removing his glasses to wipe the tears from the thick lenses.

"Even though I would love to take him home with me today, may I take him home tomorrow?" he requested. "You see, I have a few more preparations to make, and I would never consider leaving him in my car on a warm day such as this. I will need to go to a pet store to buy food and toys. I want everything perfectly in place for his homecoming."

"That would be fine," our director smiled back at him. "You

can do the adoption today and pick him up in the morning after we open."

Emmi did the adoption, which took longer than usual because Mr. Welder read the fine print in the contract, informing her of any misspelled words, grammar errors, and the structure of a proper sentence. After they completed the adoption, Mr. Welder took Rosco for a walk before leaving. After he had left, our director came to the front desk to show us the pictures of his home and the many preparations he had made to make Rosco safe.

"Have you figured out who he is?" I said, still excited over my discovery the night before.

"Yes, he's an odd man," Pat said, not even interested in my excitement.

"That man is Oliver Welder," I said, looking at everyone.

They all looked at me with indifferent, puzzled looks.

"Who?" several said in unison.

"Oliver Welder, the author," I answered back.

I could see there was no recognition on their faces.

"He is a very famous author and professor, and has written at least ten books," I told them.

They stared at me with blank looks.

"Oh, I don't read," Pat said. "Who has time to read?"

"Not me," someone else said.

"He's still weird," Pat retorted.

Exasperated, I threw up my hands. Mr. Welder, I thought, may seem weird to some people, but what hours of enjoyment this man has given through his written words.

Yes, he is an eccentric man, but with his gift of writing he describes beautiful scenes, and characterizes people, portraying them in delightful or villainous ways. A genius with words, he writes them brilliantly across the pages of his books, bringing enjoyment to his avid readers. As you read, you become part of his creative, ingenious plots and narrative.

It shows that humans, and little dogs such as Rosco who may have anomalies, flaws, or disabilities, have special gifts to give. Maybe it is only the special gift of love and protection given to a little blind dog, and then the little blind dog gives back love and companionship to a man who society thinks is strange.

A true friend knows your weaknesses but shows you your strength; feels your fears but fortifies your faith; sees your anxieties but frees your spirit; recognizes your disabilities but emphasizes your possibilities.

WILLIAM AUTHUR WARD

LILAC

The day I met Lilac, the glass on the front of her kennel was smeared where she had been licking, and then pawing at her handiwork with her front feet.

"I see we have an artist in our midst," I said while trying to see her from behind the smeared glass.

"You have been very busy," I laughed. "Are you working on a masterpiece?"

Lilac was a beautiful ten-month-old Siberian Husky. Her coat had the most interesting coloration. A light hue of gray, it almost looked blue. The blue ran up around her pricked ears and came to a point in the middle of her forehead, pointing down towards her black nose. Her face was snowy white, and the same white on her face was inside her ears, softening the blue surrounding the outer part of them. She had blue eyes, and they were expressive as she gazed intently at me. The white on her face ran down over her chest and continued down her front legs and underbelly.

Alert and responsive at our first meeting, she happily greeted me with a sharp bark and a long low howl. As most

Huskies are, I could tell she was friendly, with an outgoing personality, and ready for action.

Huskies are a breed of dog that comes frequently to the shelter. Some owners release them, but more often they have been on an adventure and animal control or a concerned citizen picks them up, bringing them to the shelter. They are high-energy dogs who need a lot of activity. Playing and socializing are important for them, and if their human leaves them home alone, they will roam to find some fulfilling entertainment. They are pack-thinking and love other dogs, needing the inter-action they receive from them. With their thick undercoats, they can stay outdoors playing in the cold for hours.

They love the snow and also water. If there is a creek, lake, ocean, or kiddie pool nearby, they will gladly wallow and splash around in it. With sheer bliss, they lay down in the water, stretching out to cool down. Used as sled dogs, they naturally have the pull instinct, so it's hard to train them to walk nicely on a leash. Their mindset is to be out front, pulling.

Watching Lilac jump onto the front of her kennel, I could tell how excited she was. I unlocked her kennel gate as she moved her tongue over the glass in anticipation. When I stepped in, she jumped down and started spinning in circles, whirling in high-spirited delight.

"Calm down, honey girl," I said, trying to put the harness on her wiggling body.

I had read her intake report, which explained why her owners had given her up. They wrote how much they loved Lilac, but she had too much energy for them, and they felt she needed a more active and structured home.

"Sit," I told her.

She sat, but still bounced up and down on her front feet. She knew she was going outdoors, and her body quivered in anticipation. I stood up straight, ignoring her excited behavior until she calmed down. She circled around me, trying to get eye contact and attention from me. When she could see it wasn't working, she sat back down with her tongue out, panting. Now she was quieter, so I clipped the lead onto her harness and opened the door so we could step out into the dog run. She plowed forward through the kennel gate, pulling me along behind her. Once outdoors, her body went into a full stretch as she pulled me toward the play yard.

When we reached the yard, I closed the gate behind us and took her leash off. Without looking back, she took off at a full run, intoxicated with her freedom. Shaking off the tenseness of the kennels inside, she circled the interior fence at a dead run, only stopping when she reached the water bowl. She took a big drink of water, and then, placing her front feet into the bowl, she splashed until the water was gone and the bowl overturned.

Looking at me for approval, she took off again, this time running in the opposite direction. I could tell she had no intention of returning, so I sat down to watch her demented lunacy. Enjoying her freedom, she continued to run her loops. A volunteer named Sam walked up to the gate to watch her. I walked over to the fence to greet him as Lilac careened and dashed past us.

"I was a musher in the Iditarod in Alaska," he said.

"I didn't know that," I responded, impressed.

"Yup, for fifteen years," he stated, shaking his head.

"Well, you are very familiar with sled dogs then," I said.

I should have guessed this about Sam. With a hardened expression between his wrinkled brown eyes, he looked as if he had been squinting for years. His face was brown and leathered, and he wore a well-trimmed graying beard. A red stocking cap always covered his head, and it matched his red and black plaid mackinaw coat. A quiet man, his mouth softened in a slight smile when he worked with the dogs. He had a no-nonsense way about him, and the dogs seemed to recognize it and wanted to please him. Expecting them to mind, he had a gentle way of earning their trust. So it was good when a dog like Lilac, who had very little training, could be paired with Sam. He watched Lilac make another flying pass before saying,

"These dogs have so much drive and energy, and are not good dogs for the faint-hearted."

"Beautiful, isn't she?" I replied.

"Yes, she has some interesting colors," he said approvingly. "How long has she been out here playing?"

"About an hour now, and she hasn't stopped yet," I answered as I watched Lilac streak past once again.

We stood talking for a while, and finally Lilac acted tired. I called her over and clipped the leash back on. Sam stepped into the play yard, and leaning down, placed her face between his cupped hands.

"My girl," he said. "You are going to be a lot of work for whoever adopts you."

She tried to lick his face, instinctively reacting to his touch.

"Do you want to take her on, Sam?" I questioned him.

"Oh, I don't know," he said. "Do your evaluation and see if she needs my skills. I'll pop into your office later to see how it went."

I should have known by the sparkle in his eyes that he knew exactly how it was going to go.

Now that Lilac seemed tired, I took her into my office to do her evaluation. After a preemptive snoop, she circled back around, prying into every nook and cranny. Stimulated by a new environment, she unleashed a good-natured chaos. Removing every toy from the toy box, she shook and tossed them wildly and threw them into the air to leap after them. After she played with every toy and scattered them around the room, she focused on the large container holding over a hundred brightly colored plastic balls.

I used this to test ball-driven dogs to see if they consistently brought back the marked ball with their scent on it I had thrown into the container. This test allowed me to know how fixated and obsessed a dog was over a ball. If a dog consistently found and brought back the right ball, I would call trainers at Boeing to see if they would look at him for their narcotic or bomb dog program. Most dogs ignored the container full of balls and preferred to play with the toys in the toy box. Lilac, however, dived in with gusto, enthusiastically plunging toward the bottom like a scuba diver looking for treasure. Balls flew everywhere around the room, landing amongst the discarded and abandoned toys on the floor.

After scattering most of the balls, she turned her attention to the container, which had flipped on its side. Circling it, she placed her front paws on the inside and propelled it around the room like a snowplow. Eventually, she flipped the open side down and jumped on top to sit and rest.

Relaxing for a few minutes, she discovered she had a higher vantage point of the room, and there were new things to be seen. Now she made the pleasing discovery of the dog food on a table. Jumping down, she charged through the toys and balls, scattering them as she ran towards the bag of dog food. I knew she had every intention of adding the dog food to the massive mess on the floor. I shot off my chair and waded through the toys and balls to beat her to her intended destination. Reaching it before she did, I snatched up the bag.

"Sit down," I demanded.

Sitting down, she wagged her tail, sending balls in a swishing wake around the room behind her. I put some of the dog food in a bowl and set it down in front of her.

Like everything else she had done, she immersed her head

inside the bowl, crunching away with gusto. Reaching down, I took the bowl from her to see if she was food aggressive. Confused, she barked at me, wanting her food back so she could finish her dinner. After eating, she must have felt freshly energized, and started looking around for her next object of interest. Pawing at the empty bowl, it turned upside down with a clang, and she used it as her newest toy. Placing her nose on the side of it, she pushed it around the room, clanging and banging it against chairs, the desk, and the file cabinet.

Eventually, she slid it underneath the bed where she could no longer reach it. Unfazed, she gazed around the room to discover the water bowl. After taking a big drink of water, I thought she would play again with the abandoned toys on the floor. To my surprise and her delight, she started splashing at the water with her front paws. Beating at it, she sloshed the water onto the walls and over the entire floor. With no water remaining in the bowl, she laid down to roll on the wet floor. Turning onto her belly, she placed her front legs under her, put her head down, and pushed off with her back feet, sliding across the floor as if on a slip and slide, leaving a runway between the cast-off toys.

Bang, she ran into the wall on the other side of the room. Standing up, she shook the water off, and then, running to gain momentum, she slid back across the room, banging into the other wall. Delighted with her new endeavor, she again turned and took another run at it, whizzing across the room. Bang, she hit the wall again.

My office looked like a wrecking ball had hit it, and with the loud thumping, crashing, and banging, Emmi came to look through the office window to make sure I was all right. Looking in, her eyes grew wide as she watched Lilac whooshing across the floor, enjoying herself immensely. I was sitting at my desk in the middle of the chaotic mess, mesmerized by Lilac's antics.

Emmi opened the door, and Lilac stopped for a moment to give her a friendly greeting before continuing her slip and slide play.

"Oh my God," Emmi said, laughing as she looked around.

"I know," I replied, frowning. "She's a free spirit, and it is going to be very hard to find a home for her."

Emmi slogged her way through the mess and sat down, looking around in amazement. There was another knock on my door, and Sam asked if he could come in. I waved him in, and he looked around with a knowing smile. Lilac was ecstatic with the added people to play with and ran over to greet Sam. Smiling, Sam pointed his hand at her and snapped his fingers. With her tongue out, panting, Lilac sat down in front of him, wagging her tail.

Sam sighed and said, "From the moment I saw you, I thought you were self-willed and out of control."

I started laughing. "I have had a lot of Huskies in my office, but I have never had one who made this kind of mess before."

Following my gaze around the office, everyone started laughing, but I was very concerned. The reality was, very few people would be interested in such a high-energy dog, who was an opportunist and ingenious at entertaining herself.

I looked at Sam. "I think we are going to need your help."

"Ya think?" Emmi said, still dazed by the mess.

"I'll take her home with me tonight, and start working with her tomorrow," Sam said. "Give me two weeks, and you will have a more disciplined dog. She will be ready for adoption with a little training."

I could tell Sam was trying to reassure me.

"Take all the time you need," I responded, looking around at the mess on the floor.

Sam kept Lilac three weeks before he told us he would bring her back. He texted me one morning asking me to remove all the toys and the container of balls before he came into my office with her. In the early afternoon, there was a knock on my door, and Sam walked in with Lilac. He told her to sit, and she sat quietly, looking around the room, not moving. He dropped her leash, walked over to a chair, and sat down. After talking with me for a few minutes, he looked over at Lilac, acknowledging her, and released her from her sit hold.

"Okay, Lilac," he said.

Only then did Lilac move from her sitting position. She calmly looked around the room and went to the water bowl to drink politely. Sam held a sack with three toys in it, and reaching inside, he pulled out the toys. Lilac happily took them from him and went to the bed to play with them.

"If you don't give her a lot of toys," Sam said, "she will be content with a few."

He told me the commands Lilac had learned, and how he had trained her to contain her energy.

"It is very important for her to have long walks first thing in the morning, and then sometime later in the day," he explained. "It is also very important that someone adopts her right away, because coming back to the shelter will trigger boredom, and when she's bored, she may resort back to the destructive behaviors she came in with."

As Sam was talking, Lilac lay on her bed with her head down, looking up at him. I kept looking at her and was amused by her reactions when Sam was not watching her. Her eyes would travel around the room, and then obediently back to him if he looked her way. I knew when given the chance, she would joyously resort to her former fun ways. I could tell she liked and respected Sam, and for him, she would control herself. But on the inside, she was still the same Lilac.

In a way, it made me feel sad to see her love of life and curiosity controlled. She was having to conform to the human restrictions of what a dog should be like, or do when commanded. Inside her, there was a free spirit waiting to break out. All it would take was the right moment or environment to unleash her pent-up energy. Dogs are opportunists and will take advantage of the moment. As long as Sam was in the room, she would abide by the rules and stay in control of herself, because she wanted to please him. He knelt down to praise her for all her hard work, and after petting her, he stood up ready to leave.

"I'm leaving for Alaska tomorrow," he stated. "I'll be back in three months."

"Thank you for helping us with Lilac," I told him. "I think she is ready for adoption now."

With a last wave, he closed the door behind him. Once we could no longer hear his footsteps, I turned and looked down at Lilac.

"I saw that look," I told her, with a knowing smile.

She thumped, thumped, thumped her tail on the floor before getting up to explore. With all the toys removed, she finally picked up one of her toys, walked over to the bed, and laid down with a resigned sigh. I knew her training would not hold out long, so I typed out her profile on the computer, describing her free-spirited personality. I hid nothing, but typed out everything, including how she was before her training with Sam. I wanted the potential adopters to know all of her behaviors, plus the skills she had learned. With the right owners, she would do great, but in my heart, I was hoping someone would adopt her with the same adventurous spirit she had. A kindred spirit is who she would be happiest with.

After closing my computer, I looked over at Lilac. She was sleeping on the bed with a toy tucked under her chin. Even though I knew she had spent time with Sam learning new skills,

I couldn't help feeling her spirit had been suppressed, so I sent up a prayer.

"Please, God, send us a nonconformist hippie, a Bohemian flower child, and a free thinker, who will allow Lilac to be herself."

A week after Lilac's return, I walked into her dog pod and noticed she was once again paw-painting on the window in her kennel. Stressed with being confined, she was reverting to the old Lilac. Even though staff and volunteers walked her, it did not provide enough stimulation for a dog as active as she was. Then we received a phone call, and hopefully an answer to my prayers. A man from upper Skagit County was calling, interested in a dog, and he was asking about Lilac.

"I am an active, single, forty-year-old man, and I work at the ski runs in the winter," he told Heather. "In the summer I spend my time as a volunteer in one of the forest fire lookouts. I loved the profile written about Lilac and had a dog like her at one time. Do you think she would be a good snowshoeing partner?" he asked.

"Yes, I think she would be excellent in any winter activity," Heather responded.

Wildly she waved at us as she pointed to the phone receiver held in her hand and mouthed,

"He wants to see Lilac."

Placing the receiver back to her ear, she asked him, "Would you like to make an appointment and come visit her?"

"I'm coming into town tomorrow to pick up some supplies," he responded. "Could I come by around eleven?"

"That would be great," Heather said. "We will see you then."

Hanging up the phone, she turned and smiled.

"He's coming to see Lilac tomorrow at eleven, and he sounds perfect."

After she told us about him, we all thought this might be Lilac's soulmate.

The next morning, I brought all the toys back into my office, including the plastic container filled with the colored balls. I felt that this man who was interested in Lilac, should understand from the beginning her enthusiasm for life. He didn't arrive at the appointed time, and we worried he had changed his mind, but he came an hour later. Heather left him in my office and went to get Lilac so he could visit with her.

When I walked down the hall, I could hear the banging, thumping, and crashing coming from my office, and I also heard a man's laughter. Knocking on the door, I stepped in. It wasn't quite the mess it had been after her evaluation, but she had still emptied the toy box and was happily lying among the masses of toys. The man stood up to introduce himself.

"Hi, I'm Winter," he said, holding out his hand.

We shook hands, and he looked at me from behind the bluest eyes I had ever seen. They were the color of the sky, and his smile was warm and friendly. His face was a healthy brown from being out in the sunshine, framed by his long graying hair pulled back in a ponytail. He was thin and athletic, and his clothes had a wood-fire scent. He carried a handmade leather beaded bag over his shoulder, and when I looked down towards the floor, he was not wearing shoes, but was barefoot.

"My free-spirited hippie!" I thought, looking down at his bare feet.

Trying to control my excitement, I invited him to sit down so I could get to know him. It was important for me to know if he would be a good match for Lilac. With a serene, philosophical nature, he told me about his job, his life, and his love of the outdoors. Lilac moved between us, busy in exploration of the office. While investigating every space, Winter watched her. Finally, he lowered himself onto the floor and called her over.

She came and sat between his spread legs while he combed her coat with his fingers. Pulling on her ears, he howled, and she joyfully joined in. Throwing back her head, she pointed her nose towards the ceiling, howling in a high crescendo to match his.

Suddenly she whirled around and went into a play stance. He got on his knees in front of her to take up the challenge. She ran around him with delighted zoomies, and as she circled him, she snatched up his leather bag, which was lying on the floor beside him. With it dangling in her mouth, she trotted off towards her bed, thrilled at claiming a new possession. He didn't retrieve it from her but laughed, unconcerned.

"She might tear it up," I told him.

"Oh, there's nothing in it she could hurt; only my billfold and phone are inside."

They continued to play together, and I was certain we had found a new home for Lilac. This man would not put a lot of restrictions on her uninhibited curious nature, and they would have many adventures in the woods, or play unrestrained in the snow. I excused myself to go talk with the director to see if she would approve the adoption. When I returned, I found them lying on the floor together as if they were having story hour.

I told him he was approved, and he could take Lilac home. We did the adoption, sending Lilac into a life where she could run free and wild with another kindred spirit. I imagined a life for her filled with sliding down mountains in the snow, splashing around in mountain lakes, and hiking in the woods. After their many excursions, they would come home to sit by a warm fire in their forest cabin. Her fur would carry the same wood-fire cologne as Winter wore on his clothes. She would live a life filled with joyous, unconfined liberty, and her spirit would not be restrained. She was going to live the life of a Husky's dream.

After they left, I looked at Emmi and said, "See, God answers prayers."

"What do you mean?" She looked at me curiously.

"I prayed for a free-spirited hippie to come and adopt Lilac," I confessed.

"Well, it looks like God answered your prayers," she said. "He certainly is a free spirit."

Then, deep in thought, she added, "I wonder if he smokes weed?"

In order to really enjoy a dog, one doesn't merely try to train him to be semi-human. The point of it is to open oneself to the possibility of becoming partly a dog.

EDWARD HOAGLAND

ROY

I will never figure out why people abandon their dogs when they could easily bring them to the shelter, with no questions asked. We have had dogs dumped on city streets, at gas stations, in other people's yards, and in city parks. Confused, they watch their owner drive away. Some people are merciless, leaving their dogs in the woods or on a desolate country road. Another animal might attack them as they forage on their own in the woods. On a country road, they could be hit by a car and crawl into the ditch, where they will die. The dog who trusted his owner for his welfare is now left behind bewildered, frightened, and disoriented. Now they will have to find a way to survive, and that is how I found Roy on a rainy Sunday afternoon.

It was late in the day when I left my house to go to my daughter's home in Snoqualmie Falls. I planned to stay the night and spend the next day with my granddaughter. As I was driving down our country lane, I noticed something black in the middle of the road. When I got closer, I could see it was a

Doberman. He was a very large dog, muscular and compact. His body swayed back and forth as if his equilibrium were off. Confused, he looked desperately around for something familiar.

I pulled over to the side of the road and stopped the car. He had a beautiful black coat that ran down the front of his legs, stopping at his ankles. His ankles were rust-colored, with two rust-colored spots on his chest. He had a long, tapered muzzle that was black on top, but his lower jaw and throat were the same rust color as his feet. His eyes were almond-shaped, and above each eye he sported rust-colored eyebrows. His ears stood cropped, erect, and alert. He was awkwardly lifting his feet, trying to balance himself.

I rolled the window down and tapped on the side of the car to get his attention.

"Are you lost?" I called out.

Trotting over to the car, he laid his enormous head on my window ledge, looking up at me. I looked around to see if any cars were nearby, but the road was empty.

"What's going on, my friend?"

I could see his hair was thin around his neck where a collar had once been.

"Did someone dump you?" I asked.

He sniffed at my coat sleeve, nudging my arm.

"What am I supposed to do with you?"

I let him sniff my hand before I pet him.

"Someone must be looking for you."

Headlights turned onto the road, coming toward us. I watched it approach, hoping it was the dog's owner. The car slowed and stopped beside me. A woman waved as she rolled down her window.

"Is that your dog?" she asked, looking concerned.

"No, I was hoping he was yours," I replied.

"No, not mine, but I noticed him earlier in the day sitting beside the road. Do you think someone left him out here on purpose?" she asked.

"I hope not," I answered.

"He's a good-looking dog. I can't imagine someone would just dump him out on the road."

She placed her hands on her steering wheel and leaned back into her seat as if to drive off.

"Well, thank goodness someone is helping him," she smiled, relieved. "I hope you will find his owner."

Waving, she rolled up her window and drove off.

I wondered how many people had seen him during the day and kept driving. Sighing, I got out of my car to open the back door so he could jump in.

"Come on," I said. "Get in."

He jumped into my backseat and sat down.

"Surely someone must be looking for you," I thought, as I got back into the car.

I watched him in my rearview mirror as he adjusted his enormous body so he could hang his head over the seat. Laying it on my shoulder, he looked at me with grateful eyes.

"What happened to you?" I said, petting the top of his head.

Because he was a purebred, I found it hard to believe someone would leave him behind on a country road. So, he must have been lost. I called the sheriff's department to see if anyone had reported a lost Doberman with his description. They told me they had received no reports of a lost dog and took all my information.

After talking with them, my only option was to take him out to the shelter to see if he was micro-chipped. It was after hours, so I knew no one would be there. If he was micro-chipped, I could call his owner to make arrangements with them to get their dog back. It was eleven miles out of my way, but at this point I had no choice.

As I drove, he circled around on the back seat and lay down to go to sleep. When we arrived at the shelter, I left him in the car so I could go inside to disengage the alarms. Grabbing a loose leash out of my office, I walked back to my car. As I approached it, I could see him sitting in the front seat, waiting expectantly for me. Slipping the loop over his head, I took him inside.

Grabbing the microchip scanner, I moved it slowly over his neck, back, and down his front legs. It was silent, with no sign of a microchip. I looked in the lost dog book to see if anyone had called the shelter missing a Doberman, but there were no entries of one.

"Okay, big boy," I said. "I am going to leave you here for the night. Hopefully, your owner will look for you and call the shelter tomorrow to see if you are here."

I knew the unexpected guest in Kennel 30 would surprise the girls in the morning. I grabbed a piece of paper to write down all the information I had about him.

"This is Roy," I wrote. "Roy is not his real name. I just named him after my dad since he seems so dignified and aristo-cratic. I found him abandoned last evening on Hickox Road close to my home. He was not wearing a collar, but it looks as if he had recently been wearing one. I scanned him for a microchip and could not find one. I placed a call to the sheriff's department to report him, and they took down all his informa-tion and where I would take him. I did not do an intake on him, so you will have to do one. I will call Emmi to let her know. If you have questions, call me. I will be back on Tuesday morning, and hopefully he will be back home with his family."

I scribbled my name across the bottom of the page and picked up the leash to take Roy to Kennel 30. I tapped the note on the glass front of his kennel and placed extra blankets on his bed with bowls of fresh water and food.

"Thank you for being such a good boy," I told him, leaning down in front of him.

Reaching over, I petted him on his head as he nuzzled into my neck. I got up to leave, and when I stepped out of his kennel, I turned one last time to look at him.

"Good night, my friend," I whispered.

I knew this might be the last time I would see him. Sometimes people get an opportunity to help one of God's creatures. Those moments imprint themselves on your heart. Helping Roy that day has been one of those moments for me.

With his owner's needless act of inhumanity, they left behind a bewildered and confused dog on a country road. "Why!"

Locking the kennel door behind me, I turned out the lights. Before leaving the shelter, I reset the alarms, and as I opened the door to my car, I heard a deep wail coming from inside the building. It tugged at my heart. Why didn't it tug at his owner's heart as they drove away, leaving him behind?

I did not return to the shelter until the following Tuesday. I was not expecting to see Roy again, but when I approached the front counter, I noticed Roy's name written on the dog board.

Surprised, I questioned Emmi, "No one came in for him?"

"No, but we got a call from a man at Lake Cavanaugh who told us he had found a female Doberman on Monday. When his wife got up in the morning, she found the dog sleeping on their deck," Emmi sighed before continuing. "He called to see if someone had lost a Doberman."

"Really! What a coincidence," I stated.

"Yes, I think so too."

"Where did you put her?" I asked.

"She's not here," Emmi said. "He asked if she could stay with them, and he was calling the shelter to give us their information in case the dog's owner called. He took her to his vet to check for a chip, but there wasn't one.

We both felt that two dogs, both Dobermans, abandoned on the same day could not be a coincidence.

"I wonder what the story is with these two?" I said.

"I don't know, but something is up," Emmi replied. "We called all the shelters in the area and animal control in different cities, with no results."

"Well, we are at a dead end for now," I said. "Hopefully, someone calls."

"Hopefully, the owners don't," Emmi replied, "because if they are abandoning their dogs on country roads, the dogs are better here in a safe place."

Standing quietly for a few minutes, deep in thought, she uttered, "Who would spend that kind of money on purebred Dobermans and then abandon them on country roads in different places?"

"There's a story behind this," I stated. "How is Roy doing?"

"He's a little aloof," Emmi told me, "but he's fine when people approach him, just reserved."

"Okay, I'll go back and take him outdoors," I said, picking up a leash and harness.

When I walked through the door into Pod L, Roy lay sleeping on his bed.

"Hello, big guy," I said, watching to see what his reaction would be.

He lifted his head in recognition and jumped off the bed.

"You remember me, don't you, my friend?"

I opened his kennel door and stepped in. There have been

Dobermans at our shelter before, but this guy was a brute and one of the largest I had ever seen. He stood at least 30 inches high and must have weighed around 90 lbs. Dignified and majestic, Dobermans are a loyal breed. They are very intelligent, making it easy to train them. Roy was happy to see me but remained calm and stately.

I slipped the harness on and fastened the leash to it. He waited patiently for me to open the kennel door before going out.

Kevin, one of our volunteers, stood at the end of the hallway watching us.

"I'm glad to see someone is taking him out," he said. "Everyone has been a little nervous around him."

"Has he acted aggressively?" I questioned.

"No, I think it's just because he's a Doberman, and maybe they're nervous because of his size," he paused. "He is rather intimidating, don't you think?"

"Well, he is huge," I responded. "One of the biggest Dobermans I have ever seen, but he seems very easy to handle."

Roy moved in front of me and sat down, leaning against me. I moved away from him so he would know I did not need his protection. One of the Doberman's traits is to claim you, and when they do, they will lean against you. Devoted, alert, and fearless, they make excellent watchdogs.

I knew by his body language Roy was claiming me and probably had from the moment I rescued him off the road. It was a good time to evaluate his temperament to see if he would show any signs of aggression. I asked Kevin to knock on my door in about an hour to see what Roy's reaction would be.

We went for a half-mile walk on the trails behind the shelter. He was excellent on a leash, with no pulling. When we got back, I took him around the other shelter dogs to see if he was reactive toward them. He smelled each dog and was friendly but disengaged from them, not interested in playing.

We visited the barn area where our feral cat community lives, and he ignored them. He was not concerned about the coming and going of our shelter workers or visitors. In the play yard he was playful, but once tired he laid down by my feet.

I brought him back indoors so he could explore my office. I thought he would lie down on the bed with toys to rest quietly. Instead, he sat down beside me with his face inches from my head, staring at me. If I got up to move around the room, he followed me closely.

He knew the commands of sit, lay down, shake, speak, go get on your bed, and leave it. He had good manners around food, and when I reached down to take his food bowl, he backed away and waited for me to place the bowl back on the floor.

When we went into the hallway with the children, he was friendly and gently took treats from their outstretched hands. Later, when Kevin knocked on my office door, he woofed to let me know someone was there but showed no signs of aggression.

After I completed his evaluation, I sat at my desk to enter everything into my computer. Roy came over and sat next to me, staring at the side of my head. Emmi knocked on my door to visit with me about another dog. Roy never moved from his spot but sat as if peering into my ear.

"What is he doing?" Emmi asked, laughing.

"Adoring me," I answered. "He has been doing it all day whenever I sit down."

She laughed louder. "Every man should take lessons from him."

"I would think something was wrong with my husband if he sat staring at me like this," I giggled, looking sideways at Roy.

I turned my head to look into Roy's adoring eyes.

"I know Dobermans are loyal, but he is taking this to a whole new level."

Emmi laughed harder as she got up to leave. She must have told staff members about Roy's adulation, because for the rest of the day they kept peering through my office window, amused and entertained by Roy's reverent gaze.

After leaving him in his kennel at the end of the day, we heard a low, unhappy wail as we went home. Emmi was touched by his loyalty and devotion, so on the days I was gone she brought him into her office so he could stare at her.

One day as Roy and I sat in the office across the hall from the front desk, a man walked by. Seeing Roy staring at me, he curiously leaned over the half door.

"Is that breed loyal?" he asked.

I turned my head to look at Roy, who sat inches away from me staring, and then turned my attention back to the man.

"Do you enjoy going to the restroom by yourself?" I asked him. "Because if you adopt this dog, you will never have another personal or private moment in your life."

He threw his head back, laughing.

"Well, I do like my privacy," he said before walking away.

Roy never flinched or moved during our conversation but just kept his steady gaze on me.

There was only one time Roy came out of his tranquil state, and when he did, it was fast and with a roar.

A man came into the shelter one afternoon upset and drunk. He spasmodically jerked his way toward the front desk, trying to stay erect. Slurring his words, he yelled at Emmi because animal control had brought his dog to the shelter.

Emmi was trying to discern what he was telling her, but was having trouble understanding him. He leaned further over the front desk, shouting at her, waving his arms. It became clear to Emmi that she could not reason with him.

Frustrated, the man reached toward her in a threatening manner.

I was working in the office across the hall when Roy came to life. Quickly, he moved toward the half door and jumped up to look over it at the drunk man.

The man had his back turned away from Roy as he boxed the air in an intimidating manner. Roy stood stiffly watching him when a rumbling growl started deep within his chest. Slowly, I stood to move toward Roy, hoping he would not decide to jump over the door before I could reach him.

Hearing the dog behind him, the man slowly turned around. Roy's jaws were now open as the growls became snarls, followed by a full-throated roar of rage. Slobber poured out of the sides of his mouth as he displayed his gnashing teeth.

Even though the man was sloppy drunk, he understood the predicament he was in. His eyes were huge with fear and glazed over as he watched the menacing Doberman in front of him. Somehow there remained enough sense in him to realize the only thing between him and the dog was a half door.

He fell back against the counter, throwing up his hands. Slowly, he started inching away toward the front door. When he reached it, he ran out of the building, running for all he was worth to the car he had arrived in.

Satisfied the man was no longer a threat, Roy turned and calmly walked back toward me. We were shocked by how quickly the whole incident happened.

Dobermans are known to be quiet stalkers and will walk silently up behind an intruder. Once close, they will startle them with a low, menacing growl followed by a very intimidating bark or roar. Startled, the intruder realizes they have just entered the wrong yard or house.

Roy easily could have jumped over the half door, but he waited to see if the man would make the right decision and leave the building. We will never know if Roy would have escalated his behavior, but what amazed me was how quickly he analyzed and controlled the situation. He knew at that moment something was wrong, and true to his breed, his natural instincts came out.

As long as he was with us, he never acted aggressively or displayed this behavior again, but of course there was no need to. When the situation was over, he calmly returned to sit next to me in his admiring, respectful stance. It was apparent Roy was fully aware of his surroundings, and his loyalty was not to be messed with.

It was not long after this incident when a couple named James and Melanie came to the shelter looking for a new dog. Their elderly dog had passed a couple of months previously, and now they felt it was time to search for a new companion to be a part of their lives and business.

They ran a winery in another county and hosted many guests who came to take part in the wine tastings. The dog they were looking for would need to be friendly and comfortable around people whom they would entertain at their events. I had heard that wineries had dogs as mascots and even named their wines after them.

Emmi directed them toward the dog kennels so they could see the dogs. After walking through each pod, they spotted Roy and came back to the front desk to learn about him. We told them why he was at the shelter and read his evaluation to them. Because they ran a winery, we also told them about the incident with the drunk man. They still wanted to visit Roy and did not seem concerned about the event.

"He has another quirk I need to tell you about," I said.

"What is that?" James asked, interested.

"He stares at you," I responded, waiting to see what his reaction would be.

"What do you mean he stares at you?" Melanie questioned me.

"Well, if you would like to visit with him, I will get him out so you can see what I mean."

I escorted them into my office and left to get Roy. When I brought him into the room, he greeted both of them. His size amazed them, and I hoped it would not be a deal breaker.

When everyone seemed comfortable, I stepped out of the room so they could get acquainted with Roy. I was gone for about twenty minutes before returning. Walking back down the hall, I could hear laughter. Looking through the window, I could see Roy sitting beside the man with his face inches away from his head, staring.

As I entered the room, Roy never acknowledged me but remained where he sat, his eyes on the man.

"This must be what you were talking about," Melanie laughed, as she pointed at Roy. "After you left," she continued, "he started staring at me, but once James called him over to pet him, Roy turned his full attention toward him and has been staring at him ever since."

James did not seem uncomfortable with Roy's gazing compulsion, only amused.

"Is this what this breed does?" James asked.

"They are a very devoted breed," I said. "But Roy, he takes it to a whole new level."

They laughed again, intrigued by Roy's eccentric behavior.

I harnessed Roy so they could take him outdoors to the play yard. When they were gone, I sprinted to the director's office to tell her about them. We watched from her office window as they played and interacted with him. He soon laid down next to them with his front feet crossed, enjoying the warm after-noon sunshine.

"What do you think?" my director asked me.

"I think they would make a wonderful home for him," I replied. "They brought pictures of their house, the winery, and their last dog. I think Roy would be happy with them."

"Well, let's give it a try," she said. Smiling, she signed their adoption application.

We sent Roy home that afternoon with his new owners, James and Melanie. They sent pictures of him, dignified and regal, surrounded by the beautiful grape vines.

When Christmas approached, we got another card. This time he was sitting between them with a red bow tie.

"Everyone loves Roy, and he is a huge part of the winery," Melanie had written. "He helps us host, and we call him the maître d', because he is the first to greet our guests with a warm welcome." Roy does not stare at us as much anymore, but he will do it occasionally. When James is working in his office and becomes a little stressed, Roy will get off his bed and come over to sit beside him and gaze. I have decided Roy thinks he is there to support James, prop him up, and to offer his comforting presence."

She signed her note — James, Melanie and Roy.

When I was through reading her note, I set it aside and sat back in my chair, thinking of Roy. I was relieved and happy he had found such a loving home, where he was loved, had a purpose, and was a part of their lives running the winery. I knew no one would ever leave him unwanted on a lonely country road again.

I thought the maître d' was perfect, but I also wondered if he had ever shown his bouncer side, ejecting a guest who had become intoxicated with too much wine, displaying unwanted drunken behavior. I probably will never know if he had, because after an incident, Roy would return to his superb maître d' manners, impressively entertaining his guests.

A dog's love is unconditional, pure, and 100% genuine. They are the epitome of true love and loyalty.

UNKNOWN

JIM BO AND JAX

IT WAS A WARM EARLY FALL, and the leaves had turned to hues of yellow, orange, and red. They had released their grip on the trees and slowly fell to the earth, covering the pathways. When cars drove by, they once again lifted off the ground as if wanting to reattach to the trees. Suspended in the air for a moment, they whirled like a ballerina doing a pirouette and then floated back toward the earth.

As I walked through the fallen leaves, I could smell their dampness and hear the crunching sound beneath my feet. It was a beautiful sunny day, and the staff and volunteers were waiting for a transfer van to arrive at the shelter. It would arrive from the state of Texas with a load of long-awaited dogs.

The Humane Society staff had made preparations all morning in the dog runs by placing bowls of food, fresh water, blankets, and a special toy on each bed. Everyone had a job to do when they arrived, whether taking the dogs out of the van or taking them to the play yard for playtime. When we brought them into the shelter, we would do their intakes, enter their information into our computers, and have a volunteer take them to their new kennels. Our goal was to calm and comfort our new residents after their long trip.

We had opened our doors to dogs from high-kill shelters in other states after hearing they were overfull and could no longer care for them. Unless another shelter rescued them, these dogs, who were arriving today, were scheduled to be euthanized. The dogs coming to us had traveled over five states to reach us. This was our third transfer, so we had become very proficient when they arrived, making the intake as welcoming as possible. We had also been very successful in finding new homes for them, which was heartwarming, knowing we had saved a life.

Around noon, the van pulled in. We opened the back doors to begin unloading the crates. Each crate held a dog: big dogs, medium-sized dogs, and small dogs. As we unloaded the kennels, we tried to communicate with each other over the noisy racket of the barking dogs. From deep within the van, I could hear the booming bay of an enormous dog.

"That sounds like a Bloodhound," I said to Heather.

She nodded her head in agreement while busily pushing kennels to the back of the van for us to lift out. Suddenly, even with all her efforts, she could not budge one big kennel. Kevin and Emmi jumped inside the van to help her. They pushed and pulled on the huge kennel, and when they finally got it to the door, it took four people to lower it to the ground. We all bent over to look inside.

I was right. A huge Bloodhound stood in the kennel, looking out at us. His eyes were hazel-colored and drooped down with heavy lids. Loose skin hung in folds on his body, and his coat was red colored with a black saddle spreading across his back. Wrinkles creased his forehead, making him appear worried, while his long, low-set ears dangled next to his flapping jowls. Bloodhounds have a very good nature and are outgoing and affectionate. People often use them in search and rescue because they have exceptional noses.

"Wow! He's a monster," Heather stated.

"Yeah," Kevin said in agreement. "I bet he weighs close to 100 lbs."

I turned his placard over to read his name.

"His name is Jim Bo," I said.

"That fits him," Kevin laughed.

Heather reached in with a loose leash, placing it over Jim Bo's gigantic head. Stepping out of the crate, Jim Bo walked with a loose gait, plodding next to her toward the play yard.

We turned our attention to the last crate in the van. This crate was quivering and gyrating across the van floor while Emmi tried to keep up with it.

"We have a live one," she yelled from within the van.

She pushed the bouncing kennel toward us, and we reached in to turn it around. Looking through the kennel gate was a white and brown Bull Terrier. An egg-shaped head held an elongated snout and black nose. His triangular eyes made him look as if he were squinting, and a brown patch circled one eye, giving him a clownish look. His ears were erect and close together, pricking forward. His white, muscular body was bouncing up and down on his sturdy front feet. He quivered with excitement, and I could tell by his high level of energy that he was ready to come out.

Bull Terriers are friendly, playful, and affectionate, but at times not good with other dogs. So, until we knew he was okay with his fellow dogs, I instructed staff to place him in a kennel by himself. I turned his placard over to read his name, which was Jax.

"Hi, Jax," I said. "It looks like you're ready to come out of there."

Holding a leash, Kevin opened the kennel door and

extended his hand inside. Jax shot out of the carrier like a missile, running for all he was worth toward the play yard. He ran through the play yard gate and lay down on the grass, rolling on his back with his legs in the air. Kevin ran after him and closed the gate behind him. By now Jax was back on his feet, zigzagging and running around the pen.

"Oh, boy!" Emmi laughed. "This guy's got energy."

We all agreed as we watched Jax somersaulting and turning head over heels inside the play yard. Kevin spent time with Jax, and when he thought he had run some of his pent-up energy off, he brought him to the building to be processed. After his intake was complete, I had a volunteer take him to the dog runs to put him in a kennel next to Jim Bo.

It took us the rest of the day to complete the paperwork, get it into our system, and place each dog on our website. Just before we left for the evening, Emmi and I walked through the dog runs to check on the new dogs to make sure they were doing okay.

When we reached Jax's kennel, it was empty.

"Where's Jax?" I said, as I looked inside the empty kennel.

"He's in here," Emmi said, pointing.

I looked inside the next kennel, and there sat Jax on the bed beside Jim Bo.

"Oh, oh," I said, concerned. "I told them to put him in the kennel beside Jim Bo, not with him. They must have misunderstood me."

"Well, they seem okay together," Emmi smiled. "But it makes me nervous until we know what Jax is like."

We got a leash and put Jax back inside his intended kennel, turned out the lights, and left for the night.

The next morning after I arrived, Kevin radioed asking if I could come to the North Wing dog kennels. When I got there, Kevin was standing by the D Pod door.

"I thought you said they were supposed to put Jax in a kennel by himself?" he asked, with a puzzled look on his face.

"I did," I said. "Emmi and I found him with Jim Bo last evening, so we put him in the kennel he was supposed to be in."

"Well!" Kevin stated as he pointed toward Jim Bo's kennel. "When I got here this morning, Jax was in with Jim Bo."

"Not possible," I said, surprised. "How did that happen? Emmi and I had found them together last night, and we put Jax back inside his own kennel. We were the last people to leave the shelter."

I walked over to Jax's kennel, and sure enough, it was empty. I leaned over to look inside Jim Bo's kennel, and there sat both dogs on the bed. Jax was sitting comfortably between Jim Bo's front legs. Both of them were relaxed and snug, enjoying each other's company.

"How did he get over that wall?" I asked Kevin.

We both stood looking up bewildered, because not only was the wall seven feet high, but a two-foot railing ran across the top of it.

"We need to set up a wildlife camera and see how he scales it," Kevin said, with admiration on his face.

"Well, he certainly must have," I stated, shaking my head. "Not once, but twice."

"Maybe they have always been together," Kevin said thoughtfully. "They really seem to like each other."

I called Emmi on her radio, and when she came through the door, I pointed at Jax's empty kennel.

"What the heck!" she said, looking stunned. "He must have climbed over the wall after we left."

"That's a first. I have never seen a dog scale a kennel wall before," Kevin said.

"There's always a first time for everything around here," I said, laughing.

Jax and Jim Bo got off the bed, stretched, and happily walked toward the front of the kennel.

"What do you think, girls?" Kevin said. "Should we keep them together?"

"We might as well, because Jax is going to jump over that wall again," Emmi replied.

"I'm glad they get along, but make sure you feed them separately until we know they are good with sharing food bowls," I instructed Kevin.

Kevin nodded his head in agreement. "I'll put Jax outside while feeding them."

Emmi and I left so Kevin could start feeding and do the morning cleaning. We went to the front desk, where the intake papers were. Looking through the pile, we found Jax and Jim Bo's paperwork. Reading through them, we could not see any notes about Jim Bo and Jax being kenneled together.

As we talked about the previous day's events, we suddenly heard Jim Bo's deep, booming bays reverberating through the North Wing and down the hall.

"He's sure noisy," Emmi said.

"I think he's missing Jax," I said, laughing.

"Listen," she said, rolling her eyes. "All the dogs are barking now."

Emmi's radio sputtered, and we heard Kevin's voice.

"Hey girls, you better come to the outside dog runs on North Wing."

Emmi and I hurried back toward the outside runs. As we turned the corner, we could see Jax running along the outside of each kennel, barking at all the dogs. He was enjoying the chaos he was creating as he ran along each fence. Dogs were running forward to bark at him, but Jax didn't care and was relishing all the mayhem he was creating.

I grabbed a slip leash that was hanging on the fence and

called Jax's name. Still running, he turned his head to look back at me, as if to say, "Do you want to play too?"

I knew he wanted us to enter his silly game. I called his name again, and he ran over, delighted we had shown up. Slipping the leash over his head, Emmi and I walked him back into the building. Kevin opened his kennel door, and Jim Bo joyously greeted him.

"I think he'll stay put as long as he's with Jim Bo," Emmi said.

We watched them wrestle with each other and then turned our attention to the fence, wondering if we could keep Jax contained. Little did we know our work was just beginning with this genius Houdini named Jax.

Over the next week we discovered Jax could easily jump anything, and he did. He climbed over the front of his kennel and into other kennels to play with his neighbors. Even with the company of Jim Bo, he would leave to go on a walkabout to meet new dogs. He seemed to have an uncanny awareness of which dogs were friendly and which dogs to avoid, skipping their kennels.

Jim Bo was content with the camaraderie and companionship of Jax, but if Jax left him behind, Jim Bo bayed his displeasure loudly.

Like an alarm, we knew every time Jax had escaped, because Jim Bo would uproariously bay out of loneliness. When we heard him baying, it was our cue that Jax was on the move. We would hurry to the North Wing dog runs to look for him.

We had learned that even when he returned to his kennel, there would be no guarantee he would stay put. More than once, a visitor, who told us they had found him loose in the hallways led him to the front. Jax had become a problem, and each day had become a day of misguided adventures, with staff trying to track him down.

We posted both dogs on our website and informed the public that Jim Bo and Jax were a bonded pair. We hoped someone would fall in love with both dogs and adopt them together. It was a lot to ask for because of the size of one and the energy of the other, but we hoped.

We were still willing to do a single adoption and soon had an application on Jim Bo. The couple met with Jim Bo, and even though they liked Jax, they only wanted one dog.

Of the two, we thought Jax would cope better with being separated from Jim Bo. We knew he would continue to crawl out of his kennel to play with the other dogs. But after Jim Bo's adoption, Jax lay unhappy and woebegone on his bed. The staff was immediately concerned because Jax, who naturally was outgoing, became very depressed.

We thought after a few days he would once again wander the halls and dog runs, but instead he would lie on his bed, sad, gloomy, and inconsolable.

A week after Jim Bo's adoption, his new owners called, wanting to bring him back.

"He won't eat," the man said, worried. "He spends most of the time in the yard with his nose in the air baying, and the neighbors are complaining. We think he misses his friend."

There was a quiet pause before he asked, "Is his friend still there?"

We allow people to return animals to the shelter if it isn't working out. We hope that the pets we adopt out will find a new family and be happy. It was obvious that Jim Bo was very unhappy, so we told them to return him.

On his arrival back, we rushed him to the dog runs to be greeted by his old friend. The two dogs were overjoyed to reunite, and we were relieved to see Jax happy again.

Soon Jax was back to himself and back to his mischievous ways. Again, he started climbing over his kennel fence to find more playmates, while poor Jim Bo bayed at being left behind.

A week after Jim Bo's return, a young couple came to the shelter interested in Jax. They took him for a walk around the shelter property and played with him in the play yard. Jax was in full form, delighted to have someone to play and show off for.

I walked down to the play yard to visit with them. After introducing myself, I told them all the information we had on Jax, even mentioning the fence climbing. I also told them how attached Jax and Jim Bo were to each other and that the staff hoped they would be adopted together.

"Is it a deal-breaker if we don't take them both?" the man asked.

"Of course not," I said. "We just know how bonded they are to one another."

"I feel bad," the man said, "but we are not prepared to have two dogs in our home."

"I understand," I told them, but felt discouraged.

Dogs are not loners and love being in a pack. So, when dogs come into the shelter after living in a home with one or two dogs, they usually need the companionship of another dog.

Being aware of this, the shelter tries to find homes where another dog is present. But as heartbreaking as it is, there are times when we have to separate dogs who have formed a special bond.

I have found over the years that dogs feel emotions and will grieve the loss of their loved ones and playmates. It can be heart-rending and traumatic for the shelter staff to watch.

The young couple adopted Jax, and he left Jim Bo behind.

He was only gone a week when we received a call from his new owner stating they could not keep Jax.

"What happened?" I questioned him.

"As soon as we let him outdoors, he takes off," the man told me.

"How far does he go?" I asked.

"Next door to the neighbors who have a Great Dane," he answered. "It would be okay if they didn't mind, but they seem to. When we're home he is okay, but if we let him outdoors or if he is home by himself, he takes off."

"Do you leave him outdoors during the day?" I inquired.

"Yes, until we can trust him," he said. "We don't want to come home to a torn-up sofa. We thought he would be safe in the backyard, but he is crawling over the fence. I'm also concerned because he is not eating well and is losing weight."

I gave the man several suggestions and encouraged him to keep trying.

"Let me know how things are going in a week."

He seemed willing to try, but it wasn't even a week before he called back. They were tired of trying to resolve the problem and decided to return Jax.

For two weeks we had listened to Jim Bo baying, and we were more than happy to have Jax come back to the shelter.

As soon as Jax arrived, we took him to Jim Bo's kennel. Happy to be reunited, they joyously greeted one another.

It was the one day that Jax stayed in his kennel. When we checked on them later in the day, they were both curled up together, sleeping in a tight, contented ball.

Jax had been back for a couple of days when one of our patrons, Lester Angilo, came to see us. Lester had adopted several dogs from us and had always preferred the very large ones.

He reminded me of Sylvester Stallone, with his jet-black hair, large nose, and kind brown eyes. He wore black T-shirts with a leather jacket, and because of his Italian heritage, I always expected to hear him say,

"How ya doin'?"

A very chatty and friendly person, he would tell us the latest stories about his dogs. So, the minute he walked through the doors, I thought of Jim Bo.

"Hi, Lester," I said. "It's good to see you."

Smiling his congenial smile, he grabbed my hand to shake it.

"Are you ready for another dog?" I asked teasingly.

His eyes filled with tears, and his smile disappeared.

"I just lost my last girl a month ago."

"Oh no! I didn't know. I'm so sorry," I told him.

"Yeah, me too."

He moved his hand over his face, trying to control his emotions.

"That's why I'm here," he said, smiling again. "Yup, looking for another dog."

I could hardly contain my excitement and hoped he might be interested in Jim Bo.

"We have a big one," I informed him.

"What kinda dog is it?" he asked.

"A big Bloodhound," I answered, looking closely at his reaction.

He started laughing before responding. "Well, I haven't had that kind of dog before. What's his name?"

"Jim Bo," I stated.

I could tell he was interested, so I told him all about Jim Bo. Because he had always had such a compassionate heart for dogs, I dropped the bombshell.

"The only problem is," I said, watching his reaction closely, "he comes with another dog. They are very bonded and love each other, so we don't want to separate them."

"Well," he quizzed me, "is the other dog a Bloodhound, too?"

"Nope, a Bull Terrier," I said enthusiastically.

His eyes twinkled in surprise and then amusement.

"Wow, a Bull Terrier!" he said. "I haven't had one of those since I was a kid."

"You owned a Bull Terrier?" I responded, excited.

"I did, and I loved him. He had a great personality with a lot of energy," he said. "How are these two with kids?" he asked. "We have a lot of grandkids, ya know."

"They have both acted nicely around children who have visited the shelter," I answered.

He stood quietly for a moment, thinking.

"I would like to meet them, and could I meet them together?" he asked.

"Of course you can," I said.

I grabbed a radio to call Kevin, asking him to bring Jim Bo and Jax up front.

"I'll help you out, sir," Kevin told Lester after he arrived with them.

"Nope!" Lester said, waving him away. "If they are coming home with me, I'd better be able to handle them."

Kevin handed him Jax and Jim Bo's leashes and walked behind them to the play yard.

I hurried into our director's office to tell her Lester Angilo was here and that he was interested in adopting both Jim Bo and Jax. She leaned over, looking out of her window to watch them.

"How many dogs does Lester have in his home?" she asked.

"None. His last dog passed away a month ago," I told her.

"Great timing, isn't it?" she said, smiling.

"It is, and he owned a Bull Terrier when he was a child."

"Well, if he's interested in taking both dogs, it would be a happy ending for all of us," she said, with relief in her voice.

Looking out her window, she reached over and patted me on the arm.

"Go on, then!" she said. "Don't you think you should go tell Lester that I approved him for both of them?"

She winked at me. "Let's get these two out of here."

I hurried out to the play yard with the good news.

"Lester," I said excitedly. "My director said she will approve you for both dogs."

"Well, let me go home to talk to the wife," he said. "I should probably think it over tonight. It's a big decision, ya know."

Disappointed he was not taking them now, I shook my head in agreement. I know two dogs are a big undertaking, so I tried to understand and be patient.

I think he could see the worry on my face, and with an uproarious laugh he reached out to give me a hug.

"How many years have you known me, Julie?" he laughed. "You have to know I'm not leaving these two behind. Go get the paperwork ready for me to sign."

I ran into the building to have Heather get the paperwork ready. When Lester had read everything thoroughly, he signed his name in big, flourishing letters.

Jim Bo and Jax were his, and they went to live in his wonderful home with many acres to run in. After they were gone, the shelter became very quiet, with no baying from Jim Bo, and we were happy not to be constantly looking for Jax.

Lester never gave the shelter a Christmas gift. His gift always came on Thanksgiving. We would receive a card with pictures of his dogs and a large donation. He told us one time he gives on Thanksgiving because his dogs are a gift, and he is very thankful for each of them.

So, in November, the card arrived with a donation, and this year a picture of Jim Bo with Jax. In the picture, they were sitting happily together, with Jax sitting between Jim Bo's front legs. Lester was also in the picture, sitting next to them with his big Italian grin.

He didn't have to say, "How ya doin'?" Because we could tell they were doing great, and because of that, we were doing great as well.

Because of the dog's joyfulness, our own is increased. It is no small gift.

MARY OLIVER

ANNIE

I was apprehensive about Annie when I first heard of her. After my weekend off, I would start the new week by gathering information on any new dogs who had come into the shelter during my absence. That morning, the staff quickly told me about a dog that had arrived the previous day.

"We have a female Pit Bull, Shar-Pei mix," Emmi stated, looking at me, worried.

I could not think of a worse breed combination for a dog, and it filled me with apprehension. Pit Bulls are a strong, confident, and fun-loving breed that has a reputation of not being good around unfamiliar dogs. They love their human families and are attentively devoted to them. The Shar-Pei breed is known to be alert, serious, and intelligent. Some people imply they have cranky dispositions. They are wary of strangers, but very devoted to their families. So, I worried about what I might encounter when I went back to the dog runs to meet Annie for the first time.

"How has she been?" I asked.

"Everyone says she has been fine," Emmi informed me.

Pat spoke up as she shuffled through papers. "Kevin told me she is very friendly."

"What is her name?" I asked.

"Annie," Emmi answered.

I walked through the dog runs, greeting each dog. When reaching Annie's kennel, I looked in, and to my surprise I was met by a cheerful, untroubled, and contented dog. She had the bulkiness of a Pit Bull, with wide, muscled front shoulders. Her coat was a rich red color with rippling wrinkles running over her body like waves. Unlike the normal Shar-Pei tail, which curls up over the back, Annie's was the straight Pit Bull tail with a white tip on the end. She swished it back and forth, back and forth, in a gentle, amiable manner.

With the many wrinkles on her face, it gave her a perturbed, worried look. Her eyes drooped as if in despondency and sorrow. Her muzzle had huge folds of skin flapping down, and when she shook her head she sent out strings of drool. The Shar-Pei's ears are very small, but Annie had Pit Bull ears. They flapped forward with the tips bending down, blending into her many folds. There was a patch of white on her chest, and her front feet had the same white, making her look like she was wearing wrinkled bobby socks.

As Annie looked up at me through her drooping eyes, she looked as if she were draped in an expensive, beautiful fur coat ready for the Academy Awards. I knew from her gentle gaze that there was something very appealing and different about this dog. I felt embarrassed about my judgmental attitude earlier in the morning.

"Good morning, Annie," I said, watching for a reaction from her.

She got off her bed, stretched, and walked toward me, with her feet making a soft plopping sound. She sat down with a grunt, leaning against the kennel door, and looked up at me with soft brown, melancholy eyes. I could feel her gentle nature and knew she wanted to be my friend.

"How are you?" I said, leaning down in front of her.

Again, she gave no negative reaction with me being eye level with her, but looked straight at me, giving a huge sigh. Because they brought her in as a stray, I could not take her out for an evaluation for three days. So, it was important to find out if the staff and volunteers could safely handle her.

I opened the kennel door to step in. Annie was delighted and ladylike in her first hands-on greeting with me. She remained calm and relaxed as I welcomed her into my world.

I was curious to see how Annie would behave when a stranger handled her. So, early afternoon, I returned to her kennel to take her outdoors for a walk. She melted into my hands as I ran them over her soft coat, petting her. Sliding my hands over her wrinkled body, I touched her front feet and then up around her neck, snapping the leash to her collar.

Her gentle nature continued to display itself as we walked past the other dogs. While they excitedly jumped and barked, making a racket, she looked neither left nor right, just slowly kept walking toward the door.

We entered the hallway and walked past the front desk. Pat leaned over the front counter to watch us walk by.

"What gear is that dog in?" she laughed.

"Low," I said, smiling back at her.

We made our way through the front doors, down the sidewalk, and started up the hill behind the shelter. Annie ambled beside me, enjoying the peaceful serenity of the woods. She traipsed along, stopping every few minutes to smell things that would only interest a dog. Checking under rocks and trees, she inhaled the rich smells from the ground. Her nose caught the scent of the dogs who had preceded her earlier in the day. Our walk was a dawdling trudge with no thought of hurry in her mind.

"Come on, sweetie," I said, trying to encourage her to walk faster.

But that was not part of her nature, and she continued to walk leisurely beside me, enjoying each and every moment.

When we went back through the front doors, there were people standing around the front counter. They had come to the shelter for business or to visit the animals. Annie, unperturbed, ignored most of them until she spotted a baby in a stroller with a small child next to it.

To my surprise, Annie came to life and tried to pull me toward the children. Not knowing what her intentions were, I called her back to me. As we walked away, she looked back at them, whining with disappointment. Still watching them, she suddenly plopped her wrinkled rear end down, determined not to leave.

"Come on, Annie," I scolded.

With a deep sigh, Annie composed herself and got up to walk away.

In that moment, I felt Annie was happy to see the two children, but I could not take a chance until I evaluated her.

When she was back in her kennel, I took the leash off and reached down to pet her. Annie ignored me and walked back to her bed to lie down with a grunt. With despondent, downcast eyes, she laid her head down on her front paws, looking at me accusingly.

If she could have talked, I think she would have said,

"How could you not let me greet those kids?"

"I'm sorry, Annie," I told her sympathetically. "But I need to test you around children before I can trust you with them."

I tried again to pet her, but she was upset with me and shut her eyes to sulk.

We learned in the coming weeks that the delight of Annie's day was to have children walk into her pod area. She went from downcast to a state of ecstasy and rapture when children were present outside her kennel. Hearing them approaching, she made a low woof or whine, trying to draw their attention toward her.

She would lean her body against the front of the kennel so they could reach their little fingers in to pet her. Stretching out her black tongue, she affectionately licked them. Then, with a sudden burst of energy, she would zoom around the kennel, causing the children to laugh delightfully at her funny antics.

Annie had passed her evaluation with high marks, and she would be a great match for a family. So, I was surprised and disappointed when our director told me she would not consider Annie for a family home with children.

"Annie loves children," I told her. "She is depressed when she is not around them."

Sympathizing with me, she answered back. "Nevertheless, we have no background on this dog, and I can't take a chance."

I protested, but she put her hands up, looking at me relentlessly. "With the two breeds she is mixed with, I can't take a chance."

I could tell she had made up her mind with no intention of changing it. I understood why she was concerned about the prospects of putting these two breeds into a family environment, but Annie adored and loved children.

With no children in Annie's future, the staff felt disheartened and sorry for her.

"Well, maybe the new owners will have grandchildren," Emmi consoled me.

"This is so unfair," Pat said, wiping tears from her eyes.

Pat's tears surprised us, because she was always the logical, tough one of the staff, pummeling us with her outspoken views.

At the shelter, people can get pre-approved while they are in search of a pet, such as Greg and Becky were. They watched our website closely and would visit the humane society when they found a dog they were interested in.

When Greg and Becky read about Annie, they thought she would be the perfect fit for their home. Driving over to the shelter, they wanted to meet her. After visiting her, they fell in love and wanted to adopt her.

We knew they were young and inexperienced with dogs, but they had done their homework, reading about the two breeds Annie's was mixed with. They told us they loved their careers and had chosen not to have children.

Both worked away from home during the day, but they explained how they would use toy stimulation, with long morning and evening walks together. They had already interviewed a dog walker to take Annie out in the middle of the day.

They rented a condominium close to a dog park, and their condo association allowed dogs, but only quiet dogs. Their home had a doggy door, which led to a small outdoor area enclosed by a fence. Annie could come and go as she pleased while they were away during the day.

They loved Annie's pleasant personality and were intrigued by her soft coat, calling her their wrinkled beauty. We were pleased with all the research they had done and how they had prepared for a dog. This was a perfect placement for Annie, except there were no children.

After her adoption, we heard nothing from them for two months. Then, on a Saturday morning, they walked into the shelter. The staff thought they were there for a visit, but the moment they saw them, they knew something was wrong. Becky started crying, with Greg standing behind her, dejected and downcast.

"Where is Annie?" Emmi asked.

"She's still in the car," Greg answered.

"We have to bring her back," Becky said, between sobs.

Emmi pulled some tissues from a box, handing them to Becky.

"What happened?"

"We can't keep her home, and she is so unhappy," Greg answered. "We live near a school, and the first week she got out of our yard. She went to the school to play with the kids, and of course the teachers didn't want her there and called animal control. After reading her tags, the animal control officer called us to come pick up our dog."

Greg rubbed Becky's back, trying to comfort her.

"That was the first week she was with us. We thought once she adjusted to our home, she would settle and become more content. But two days later we got another call from animal control telling us she was once again at the school. She asked us to pick her up and threatened us with a fine if she returned."

"How far is the school?" Emmi asked.

"That's the problem," Greg answered. "It is only a block away from our house."

"So we tried to keep her home by securing the fence," Becky sniffed. "We thought there was no way she could ever get out again."

"But two days later," Greg continued, "the school called us again to tell us Annie was there, and could we come get her. When I arrived, it was obvious the teachers liked Annie and did not want to involve animal control again. So I reassured them I would find a way to keep her home."

"We tried doggy daycare for two weeks," Becky interrupted. "The people there told us she was unhappy and would not play or interact with the other dogs. She would only lie on her bed, depressed. They were worried because she had started sleeping all the time."

"So we stopped taking her to daycare," Greg sighed.

"Now," Becky interjected, "I had the idea of closing the dog door in the condo to leave her indoors all day. We thought things were going fine until our neighbors started calling to complain about Annie's howling."

"I have never heard her howl or even bark," Greg said indignantly. "But the complaints kept coming, so we left our condo on a Saturday morning and stood outside the door to listen. There was not a peep out of her."

Becky shook her head in agreement.

"We have great neighbors, and we knew they were not complaining for no reason. So Greg set up a camera so we could watch her on our phones. Sure enough, on Monday morning she stood next to the door and howled. As we watched, Greg noticed she howled for a while and then would lie down.

Then he became aware that she was going to the door and howling at certain times. She howled at 8:00 a.m., 10:00 a.m., 12:00 p.m., 2:00, and again at 4:00. Then she was quiet until we reached home."

"Now we knew," Greg said, smiling. "She howls when the children are coming to school in the morning, at both recesses, noon break, and when they leave in the afternoon. All other times she is quiet."

The shelter staff stood intrigued by their story while they continued to talk.

"The condominium association has cooperated with us as we have tried to resolve this problem, but now they have lost patience. They told us we had a week to address the issue with Annie, or they would ask us to move.

Becky started crying again. "So we have no choice, and we have to bring her back."

I was not there the day Annie was brought back to the shelter. The following morning, I looked at the board and was startled to see her name listed.

"Is that our Annie?" I asked, surprised.

Emmi sadly shook her head up and down and began recounting the story to me.

Once again, we posted Annie on the website and began searching for a new home for her. She lay lethargic on her bed unless children came into her pod. Then she would joyfully jump up, energized by their presence.

Within a week, our director found her another home. This time with a retired couple who lived in the country.

"This is Marjorie and Stan's application," she said, waving it in the air. "It's a beautiful home, and it will resolve the problem of kids because they have grandchildren."

She held the pictures up for me to see. "So Annie can get her kiddo fix whenever they come for a visit."

Looking at the pictures, I could see it was a lovely home, but I had a feeling small doses of children would not fulfill the need Annie had for them.

The new couple came to adopt Annie several days later. This time Annie was gone for three weeks before being returned.

The day Marjorie returned her, she sadly stated that their grandchildren had come for a visit on two separate weekends, with everything going well until the children left.

"When they leave," Marjorie told us, "Annie will sit by the door and howl, and I cannot stand it any longer."

She continued talking as she squeezed her hands in frustration. "Her heart is broken, and I will not be a part of it because Annie needs children."

She folded her arms in front of her, taking an unyielding stance. I could see Annie had a determined advocate in this woman, who was willing to crusade for her need to have children as a part of her life.

While we stood listening, we could tell Annie's new owner had no intention of backing down from her position.

"I would like to talk to the director," she demanded. "I want to question her about why Annie is not allowed to be with children."

Our director had overheard the conversation from her office and came out to speak with her. Marjorie again repeated the story, asking her to reconsider her position.

"Annie loves children and would never hurt one," she pointed out. "I would try to find a home for her with kids, but I signed an adoption contract stating I would bring her back to the shelter if there was a problem."

Holding her hands up, exasperated, she said, "Well! There's a problem! A big one, and Annie needs to be with children."

By now her voice had elevated. "I want you to find a home with kids so Annie can be fulfilled and happy," she said.

Our director lifted a hand, relenting. She now realized after adopting Annie to two different homes with people telling the same story, it was clear to her that Annie needed a home with children.

"I agree with you," she said. "It is obvious Annie loves children and would never hurt one. So yes, we will find a home for her with kids."

Once again Annie was returned, but this time we were all happy and relieved, because now we would look for a home where children were present.

Annie once more took up residence at the shelter. I was relieved, knowing we would look for a home where Annie would be happy. Once placed, she would live out her life surrounded by children.

She had been back at the shelter two weeks when a family with three children came in looking for a dog. I spotted them from the end of the hallway and directed them to Pod B, where Annie was.

Checking on them later, I walked through the door to see the children admiring her. They were reaching their little fingers between the bars to touch her soft coat.

I told the parents how much she loved children and about the last two adoptions. They wanted to take Annie to the play yard to get better acquainted with her.

Leaving them there, I went back inside the shelter to my director's office. We stood at her window watching the children play and interact with Annie. She cuddled with each child and happily followed them as they ran around the yard.

We could hear the children calling her name and their laughter when she ran over to them.

One of the little boys fell while running. Annie was immediately concerned and ran to his side to make sure he was okay. The mom picked the crying little boy up to nestle him in her arms. Annie moved close to snuggle next to them, licking the boy's face.

When I returned to the play yard, the dad smiled as he pointed at Annie and his kids.

"We love her and would like to adopt her," he said. "The deciding moment was when Annie was so gentle with Josh when he fell down."

I took them back indoors so they could complete the adoption.

When the time came for them to leave, each child came to hug the staff. It was wonderful to watch Annie leave the humane society that day with her new brood.

The family lived in another city, so it was unlikely we would ever see her again. Happy for Annie, we watched her wagging tail as she jumped inside the car with her new family. Waving goodbye, we could see her in the backseat among her children.

With smiling faces, they all turned to wave, except Annie, who never looked back.

We always receive pictures and cards from the people who have adopted from us around Christmas time, but we did not hear from Annie's family for two years. When a letter finally came, a picture dropped out, floating down onto the countertop.

It was a picture of Annie surrounded by her family of children. There was also a note, which read.

Dear Shelter Staff,

I am writing to tell you what a wonderful dog Annie has been for our family. She melded into our home as if she had always been here. I can't imagine someone had given her up, and I can't imagine life without her.

When we brought her into our home, we thought a good place for her to sleep would be in the laundry room. Like Annie fashion, she did not fuss, but when we got up the next morning, we found her in the upstairs hall close to the children's bedroom door.

We tried again the next evening, putting her back in the laundry room. We were trying to establish where she should sleep at night, but as soon as she thought we were sleeping, we could hear her coming up the stairs to lie down in the hallway.

We soon gave up and placed her bed outside the children's door. There she contentedly slept through the night. If something happened, or there was a need with one of the children, Annie would alert us to tell us something was wrong.

Soon after we adopted her, I found out I was pregnant. In January, we welcomed another baby boy into our family. Annie was delighted and adored him.

She took up a new post under his crib at night. She worried if he cried or squirmed and would come into my room to wake me.

She did not forget the other three children as they played indoors or outside. She played and romped with them, but once tired, she would post herself on the porch where she could monitor them, making sure they were safe.

If one of them got into a little trouble and had to sit in the corner, she would sit alongside them. If they cried, she howled. If they fall and hurt themselves, she runs to alert me and insists I check on them.

She loves all children, and they are all safe with her. While my friends and I visit inside, she is our watchful babysitter. We never worry about their safety or well-being because Annie is always close by.

Tragedy struck our home in the early spring of last year when my husband lost his life in a car accident. As my children and I mourned through those dark days and months, we had to learn to adjust to a life without him.

Annie became our rock while trying to comfort us. I would watch out the kitchen window to see one of the children with their arms around Annie's neck, crying into her soft, wrinkled folds.

Because I needed to stay strong for my kids, I cried into her folds at night. Annie coaxed us through this last year, nurturing us to move forward.

A lot of healing has taken place, but there are days when it is overwhelming. Annie and I are parenting together. We are a team raising four adorable children, who are starting to laugh again.

Thank you for bringing Annie into our lives. She came to us at the perfect time. My parents coined a new name for her. They call her Nanny Annie.

We cannot imagine life without her. She is our treasure, and I wanted you to know how loved and adored she is to each member of our family.

Love, The Patel Family

The gift I am sending you is called a dog, and is the most precious and valuable possession of mankind.

THEODORUS GAZA

MOOSE

One thing I always said to the staff and volunteers at the shelter was, "You can think like a dog, but a dog can't think like a human."

Example: Moose, a one-year-old German Shepherd, was brought to the shelter because he had killed some of the neighbor's chickens. German Shepherds are a beautiful breed, powerful and intelligent. They are also known to be guardians and can be protective of their owners and property.

So, in Moose's logical dog mind, how was he to know when to protect the property where he lived, and from whom? How was he to understand that the neighbor's chickens were somewhat innocent, with a natural tendency to wander? At what point after he noticed them did he know these chickens might be allowed full reign in the neighborhood, including his yard?

To his understanding, these unfamiliar beings had just shown up. He watched them from his back porch, crossing the road from the neighbor's house. Boldly, they ducked under the fence into his yard and then began to tear up his owner's flower beds.

What was a fella supposed to do? Is he supposed to watch and do nothing as they blatantly steal the insects off his property? Not on his watch; it ain't happening.

Later when the owners returned home, they noticed their neighbors searching for some missing hens. Entering their backyard, Moose happily greeted them. As they looked around, they could see where the neighbor's hens were, and the evidence of Moose's afternoon enterprise, with feathers lying all over the grass.

How was he supposed to know they were harmless? What he didn't know was that they were chickens with chicken brains, and he was a dog with a dog brain. His brain told him they were intruders, and so he reacted.

The neighbors did not want to secure their property to keep their chickens in a safe environment. They thought it was okay for their clueless hens to nibble their way wherever they chose to go. Now they wanted Moose gone, telling his owners he was a vicious dog, and they were calling animal control.

The owners did not want a dispute with their neighbors or involvement with animal control. So now they were standing in front of us, wanting to release their dog.

"Our neighbors do not like our dog," the Hispanic man said.

His children clung to his pant legs while they looked up at us with sad brown eyes wet with tears.

"You must find a better home for him, because he is a good dog," the father continued.

Our director, overheard him speak in broken English, came out of her office to talk with him in Spanish. She gathered as much information as she could about the dog and translated what he was saying to us in English.

"He is a friendly dog," the man said. "His name is Moose."

"Moose," I said, looking over the counter at the huge German Shepherd standing next to the man.

When he heard his name, his ears pricked forward, attentively watching me. He had a beautiful brown coat, with a black saddle spreading over the top of his back. With his impressive size, I understood why they called him Moose.

Observant and focused, he was concerned about his crying children and paced back and forth between each child. Because the children were upset and crying, I knew Moose was feeling stressed.

In all the confusion, I did not want to pick up his leash and walk away with him. I asked the father if he would walk Moose back to the dog runs with me.

I didn't want the children to see or experience Moose being placed inside a kennel and having to leave him behind. So I requested they stay in the lobby with their mother.

Moose happily walked beside us, and once inside the dog runs, the father put him into a kennel. He took the leash off and bent down to affectionately tell him goodbye.

Stepping out, he shut the gate behind him and looked back at Moose with misgivings.

I reached out to touch his arm. "I promise you," I told him, "we will find Moose a good home."

"Yes, yes, he is young, he is a wonderful dog," he said, wiping away a tear. "Please call me when he is in his new home, then I can tell my children he is doing well."

"Yes, we will call you," I told him.

Moose sat behind the closed gate watching us closely. Confused and bewildered, he started whining at being separated from his owner, who was walking away.

When we came back through the dog wing doors, the owners' children looked mystified at not seeing Moose with their father. He bent down to gather them into his arms and gently hug them. He tried to tell his little ones why Moose wasn't with him and why the shelter needed to keep him until they found a new home.

They cried pitiful tears while clinging to him. The man and his wife took each child by the hand and led them out the doors. One little boy looked back at us with puddles of tears running down his face, calling,

"Moose, Moose."

It broke our hearts as we watched them leave.

"Poor little guy," I said, feeling awful.

Irritated, Pat ranted. "I think when I get home tonight, I'm going to eat chicken. Yup, fried chicken, a big plate of it."

The next day, I went to get Moose out for a nice morning walk and establish a relationship with him. Taking him outdoors into nature would get him away from the noise of the kennels and help with any stress he was feeling.

He walked well on the leash, staying close beside me. We strolled up the hill behind the shelter, taking in the sounds and smells of the woods.

While we walked, he relaxed and became interested in his new surroundings. He did not seem overly anxious with his new circumstances, which is unusual for this breed.

My biggest concern for a dog who is released by his owner is depression. Our goal at the shelter was to make it as stress-free as we could, with routines.

Using nature as a healer was significant and normal in the dog world. We walked among the trees, with the birds singing their morning songs and the sun warming us.

In this stress-free habitat, Moose was surrounded by nature in all its freshness.

When we first started our walk, Moose avoided eye contact with me because I was a stranger to him and not a part of his pack. But as we walked, he soon relaxed and began to trust me.

I found a log to sit down on, and after smelling around, he sat down beside me, leaning against my leg.

Reaching down, I ran my hand down his back, petting him.

"Isn't this sunshine nice?" I said.

He looked back at me with soft brown eyes, his tongue out, panting.

"You really enjoyed this, didn't you?"

I knew after trekking up the hill for a few days, we would become good friends, and Moose would be ready for his evaluation. At that time, I would introduce him to Richard.

Richard was the roving rooster, who ruled the shelter grounds with iron talons. He roamed the shelter property with the nobleness of a king. Setting his no-nonsense rules, he was feared and respected.

A Rhode Island Red, he came to the shelter in a cat crate. After we searched and could not find an owner, we transferred him to the barn with the hens, naming him Richard.

He immediately tried to impress them by showing off. Puffing out his chest with self-importance, he marched around the barnyard. He seemed to enjoy their company, but soon expanded his kingdom to the other shelter buildings, which included the dog runs.

I think he thought the dogs were part of his harem, and another place to rule. We also discovered he was cranky with some dogs who did not respect his boundaries.

Each morning, he paraded around the outside of the dog runs, crowing his raspy revelry. Bugling at full attention, he made sure none of his rules had been broken during his absence.

Once satisfied all was well, he pecked nonchalantly through the surrounding flower beds for bugs.

Most dogs detected his crankiness, but we had a few who had to learn the hard way.

Even though we warned people about Richard's fractious nature with dogs, a few had to experience it while taking a dog out for a walk.

As I was getting out of my car one afternoon, I noticed one of our volunteers walking a dog. Seeing Richard, she walked toward him, pointing, and said,

"Look, Fido, a chicken."

Richard, seeing them approaching him, stood at his full rooster height, fluffed out his feathers, and started flapping his wings. I could see what was about to happen, but before I could give a warning, Richard started running toward them.

Sprinting at full speed, he beat his wings while screeching a rooster war cry. He chased the scared woman, and even more frightened dog, toward the shelter doors.

Staff members, hearing the commotion, ran outside waving towels, trying to stop the ensuing battle, which he intended on fighting.

Seeing the towels waving in the air, he stopped, but still mad, he stomped around like an incensed prizefighter.

Flapping his wings, he let out a loud crow trying to shake off his mad.

Because of these incidents, we placed signs on all the exterior doors warning volunteers and visitors that when walking a dog, do not approach the resident rooster.

But there were always a few who did not believe us and had to learn the hard way.

Richard and I formed a working relationship. When he knew I was inside the play yard with a dog, he would come over to roam around the outside of the fence to make his presence known.

While the dog and I played, he would peck through the grass, acting nonchalant and unconcerned.

Even though they noticed him, most dogs' attention was on

me. If they became interested in him and ran toward the fence, Richard would charge toward them, meeting his aggressor with full force.

Usually, the dogs were surprised by this response. Bewildered, they would run back toward me looking for comfort and safety.

Scolding the dog, I would tell it to leave the chicken alone.

If Richard recognized the dog was no longer a threat, he would move away and continue his hunt for bugs.

But every once in a while, he met a dog who had no intention of leaving him alone. Then Richard would go into full battle mode, and like a covert combatant, he waited for the dog to charge the fence.

With a calculated move, and claws fully extended, Richard jumped, reaching through the fence to dig his talons into the dog's soft nose.

Surprised at the ferociousness of the attack, and in pain, the dog yelped. Hurling himself backward, he would run back toward me.

It was a tough lesson to learn and did not happen often. But when it did, it became a lifelong deterrent for the dog.

With respect now established, Richard strutted off knowing he had made his argument about why dogs should leave chickens alone.

After one of these encounters, the dog would keep a watchful eye out for chickens and avoid them.

Sometimes, they had to learn this lesson more than once, but that was very rare.

On the afternoon that I was doing Moose's evaluation, I walked him down to the barn area to meet the chickens.

It did not take him long to spot them, as they happily pecked their way around the barnyard. His body stiffened, and his ears pricked forward with interest and excitement.

Suddenly, he lurched, clawing his way toward them, pulling hard on his leash. Squawking and cackling, they ran in every direction, causing a ballyhoo.

This energized Moose even further into an excited state of madness. With his chicken drug accelerating through his veins, he jerked the leash from my hand, giving chase.

He was so focused and delighted; he failed to notice Richard, who, at hearing all the commotion, had appeared in the barn doorway.

As the hens ran and flew toward the safety of the barn, Richard stepped out, preparing for battle.

Head high, feathers extended out around his neck, he pushed his chest forward and crowed his battle cry.

Stomping his feet, he stood his ground while the hens ran past him.

He let out another mighty crow and lowered his body to prepare for the oncoming fight.

When Moose saw him, he stopped for a moment, unsure, and looked back at me. I tried calling him, hoping he would come back.

Richard once again flapped his wings, giving another call for battle, and at that moment, Moose decided to give chase.

When he reached the doorway, Richard was already in the air, landing in the middle of his back.

With his talons dug in, he pecked hard on Moose's neck, flogging him with his wings.

Moose yelped in surprise and pain. Spinning in circles, he tried to dislodge Richard from his back.

I could hear his teeth snapping as he reached back, trying to bite at his formidable adversary.

When he realized he could not dislodge him, he started running for the safety of the main building.

Halfway there, Richard flew off his back, but still continued to fly over him.

As soon as Richard could see his enemy in full retreat, he turned away and landed.

Swaggering, he strutted proudly toward the barn.

Pat had just returned from lunch and was standing by the front doors when all this took place. Seeing Moose at a dead run toward her, she opened the doors so he could run in.

When I reached the main building, Moose was under a desk, trembling with fright. Nervously, he looked behind him, terrified Richard would show up any moment.

Pat and I knelt down to sympathize with him, checking him for wounds.

Even though we felt sorry for him, we could not help but laugh at the whole incident.

"That's one mean rooster, isn't it?" I said.

"Yes," Pat agreed. "You'd better leave the chickens alone."

Once Moose was less frightened, I put him in my office where he felt safe.

After his chicken experience, Moose did not want to go anywhere near the barn.

He did eventually venture closer, but drew a firm line in the grass about midway.

Carrie and George were wonderful volunteers who spent two days a week walking dogs. Both were retired and had owned dogs in the past. Now they wanted to travel and did not want the responsibility of owning one.

The day they came across Moose in the dog runs, they asked if they could start walking him.

George, a retired pilot, had startling blue eyes true to his Norwegian heritage. Well over 6', he stood as if standing at attention, a formality he had learned from serving in the Air Force.

He was serious by nature and wanted to follow the requirements the shelter had set for walking dogs.

I liked this because Moose needed a strong, disciplined person who was going to set some firm rules.

Carrie, a retired nurse, was small and petite for her size, looking undersized next to her husband.

She was outgoing and friendly, with permanent laugh lines around her mouth and eyes.

She was the nurturing type with a carefree way. With her cheerful nature, she would motivate and encourage Moose.

I loved their combination of personalities and teamwork, and it wasn't long before we noticed they were coming in extra days to walk Moose.

Because of their hard work, Moose was soon ready for a new home. We posted him on our website and opened the application process for him.

Many people showed interest and filled out applications, but most of them did not have shepherd experience, or worse yet, owned or lived near chickens.

"Don't you think he has learned his lesson?" Pat said one afternoon, throwing down the applications on the table in front of her.

"We just can't take a chance," our director stated. "If he lost his mind when encountering a chicken, he may have to come back, and we don't want that to happen."

So we kept going through applications looking for a perfect home for Moose.

One afternoon, after Carrie and George walked Moose, they approached us wanting to adopt him.

Confident this was a perfect placement for Moose, we adopted him to them the following day.

After Carrie and George adopted Moose, their time spent walking dogs at the shelter dwindled.

When they came in, they were guilt-ridden and tried to explain why they were not there as often.

We understood Moose was taking more time and energy from them. This often happened after volunteers adopted a dog.

Even though we missed them, we wanted them to love and nurture their new family member.

Reassuring them it was okay, we encouraged them to take part in some of the other volunteer programs.

George and Carrie continued to support the shelter by volunteering in fundraising. We were delighted with all their help, and even more delighted to see Moose.

One day, George came into the shelter with news that they were moving to Portland. In Portland, they would be closer to their children.

The day before they left, both George and Carrie brought Moose in to say goodbye. Giving Moose a farewell pat, I thought it would be the last time I would see him.

A year after their move, George and Carrie pleasantly surprised us when they came in to see us with Moose.

"He looks wonderful," I told George.

"He really has worked out well for us," George answered back. "He is a good dog with good manners, and we can take him anywhere."

I smiled while stroking Moose. "Has he seen any chickens?"

"No one in our neighborhood has any," George laughed. "We live right off the beach, so all he encounters are people and dogs."

"Well, that's good. We wouldn't want any temptations," I smiled.

Another year passed before George and Carrie were back for another visit. During the time they spent with us, Carrie told me she had a degenerative eye condition and was slowly going blind.

"I'm so sorry," I sympathized with her.

"I know, but the good news is, Moose is in training to be my seeing-eye dog."

"They can do that?" I questioned her.

"Yes, and he is doing great in the training program."

"Well, Moose," I said, reaching down to pet him, "who would have ever guessed."

The staff all made over Moose and were thrilled to hear of his new training as a seeing-eye dog, which would be a blessing for Carrie.

Two years went by before we saw George and Carrie again. On the day they came in, Moose was in full harness. It was obvious to all of us that Carrie was now blind and dependent on Moose for her eyes.

It saddened us to see Carrie like this, but we felt pleased to see Moose with such a purpose.

After we spent some time visiting, George approached me and took me aside.

"Moose is remarkable," I said.

"Yes, when we adopted him, we never imagined he would become a seeing-eye dog for Carrie," George smiled.

"I am so glad he has worked out like this," I smiled back.

George shook his head in agreement and then furrowed his brows, looking at me closely.

"You know," he said hesitantly, "he has been a great dog, but I have something to tell you."

I looked at him, interested, ready to hear about some heroic act Moose had performed.

"I always let him out first thing in the morning," he said, lowering his voice, leaning closer to me. "About two weeks ago, after he had been outside for a while, I opened the door to let him back in, and on my front porch was a dead seagull."

He looked at me intently to see what my reaction was before continuing. "There were feathers everywhere," he whispered.

I lifted my eyebrows in surprise, watching the perturbed look on George's face.

"Do you think Moose killed him?" I said quietly.

"Well, either he killed him, or found him dead somewhere out on the beach," he whispered back.

"What did you do?" I asked.

"I got a garbage bag and bagged it, feathers and all. All the time I stuffed that bag, I hoped our neighbors were not watching," leaning even closer, he continued. "Then I walked to the garbage bin and threw it in."

He looked at me with a tormented look, and at that point I started to giggle.

"Do you think he was avenging Richard?" I asked, still whispering, trying to suppress a laugh.

"I don't know," George said, perplexed. "As I was picking up feathers, Moose sat there watching me, with a panicked look. I think he thought the thing might come back to life."

I could no longer contain myself. "Poor seagull," I laughed.

Fidgeting, he reached out and took my arm. "Don't mention it to Carrie," he said, still in a whisper. "She doesn't know."

I shook my head up and down, assuring him I would keep his secret.

During the rest of their visit, I chuckled when I looked at George or Moose.

When the time came for them to leave, we followed them to the parking lot.

As George opened the car door, I noticed Richard happily scratching through the flower beds about twenty feet away.

Moose also spotted him and gave a horrified look of fear.

With Carrie hanging onto the harness, he did not break his hold and performed his job proficiently, but nervously kept watching Richard.

George helped Carrie get into the car and put Moose in the backseat.

Looking back at me, he smiled, giving a thumbs up.

When he walked around the car, I gave him a hug, patting him on the shoulder.

"By the way he looked at Richard," I whispered, "I bet that seagull was already dead."

George shook his head in agreement.

"Well, we'll never know for sure," he commented. "After seeing Moose's reaction at seeing Richard, I hope it was a good reminder for him."

When their car drove out of the parking lot, I noticed Moose looking back at us from the rearview window, or maybe it was Richard he was watching.

You can think like a dog, but a dog can't think like a human.

JULIANN BISTRANIN

JACK

He looked at me from behind the kennel bars, and if I moved too quickly, he raised his head, showing his teeth. Jack was an Australian Cattle Dog, or what some people refer to as a Blue Heeler.

"What has made you so mad, my friend?" I commented in a quiet voice to comfort him.

His head dropped down onto his paws, and I continued to talk quietly to him. I knew he was confused and might bite if given the chance. I love the Blue Heeler breed. They are focused, intelligent dogs with an independent spirit. Hard-working, they have two loves: their owners and their jobs. I had experienced this breed with my Blue Heeler, Jazzy, and had grown up around them in Montana. They are one-person dogs and can be cranky, with a propensity to bite, especially in a stressful situation such as this.

His family had surrendered Jack the day before. His owner told Heather they had gotten him as a puppy, but after bringing him home they realized they did not have the skills or knowl-edge to keep him content. They had him for around six months when he displayed his quirky personality. Bored, he found jobs around the house to release his pent-up energy. He had recently started focusing on the mailman, who was feeling threatened, and because of this his family felt they could no longer keep him.

"He won't deliver our mail because he's afraid Jack will bite him," the woman said. "Jack has never bitten, but our mailman says Jack is showing his teeth."

"What have you done to keep him busy?" Heather questioned her.

"Well, we are a very busy family," she said defensively. "So he has to stay in the yard while we are at work, or at the kids' activities."

"I understand what you are saying, but this breed has high energy and needs something to do. If they don't have a job, they will create one."

Heather felt sorry for Jack, because he had been living in a home with no understanding of the Blue Heeler breed.

"I know," the owner said. "I knew we were in trouble when we got home recently, and he had torn the siding off the lower part of our house, and had placed it in a neat pile in the middle of our yard."

"Yes, they are known to be a demolition crew," Heather said, laughing.

"We feel so bad," the woman said, with tears in her eyes. "I think he would be happier on a cattle ranch, or at least somewhere where they will have more time for him."

"Yes, I agree with you," Heather told her. "So we will try to find him a working home."

After his owner left, Jack whined because he could not understand why she had left him behind. Turning his attention to Heather, he showed his teeth, warning her to keep away. She carefully picked up his leash so she could take him through the dog runs to his kennel. He let her take the leash off with no attempt at biting, and with a depressed wag of his tail, he walked over to the bed and laid down with a bewildered sigh.

After reading his paperwork, and because he was giving warnings with his teeth, I knew I would have to find a safe way for the staff to handle him.

The next morning I went into Pod E and stood outside of his kennel. He was lying on his bed, looking lonely and depressed. Sitting down on the floor, I spoke softly to him. Every time I looked at him, he lifted his upper lip, showing his teeth, but he never growled.

"Somehow," I whispered to him, "we need to come to an understanding, with one of us compromising."

He showed his teeth again while I continued talking.

"You need to be nice, my friend," I said softly, "because we need to be able to take you out without you hurting one of us."

The longer I sat there, the more he seemed to relax. After a while, he slowly belly-crawled toward the front of the kennel. With a huge sigh, he put his head down on the floor and looked up at me.

"Good," I said, still not giving him eye contact. "I would love to take you outdoors."

I slipped a treat under the fence so he could smell it. After a few minutes, he stretched his neck out, picking it up to eat, but when I looked at him, he again showed a quick flash of teeth. If I looked away, he would lay his head back down on his front paws and sigh.

Look, flash. Look, flash.

He continued to show his teeth whenever I glanced at him. I tried yawning, thinking it would help him relax more, and he yawned back. He was watching my hand, looking for another treat, so I slipped another one under the kennel fence. His nose started moving, and leaning way forward, he stretched out his neck to pick it up. He chewed it up, swallowed it, and begged for another treat.

As I watched him, I noticed his eyes did not have a hard stare as an aggressive dog would display. Instead, his eyes remained soft, but he was still flashing his teeth.

I moved closer so I could lean against the kennel bars. He crawled to where I was seated and turned over onto his back, exposing his belly. He waved his paws in front of him, pawing at the air playfully.

Suddenly, I understood what he was communicating.

"You're not showing your teeth out of aggression, are you?" I said, laughing. "You're smiling."

As the dog evaluator, I had learned there were different reasons for dogs to show teeth, and it was not always from aggression. It may be because they were nervous, or because of excitement, but whenever you see a mouthful of teeth, people take it as a warning to stay away. Why Jack had learned this quirky trait, I could not say.

Maybe he was nervous, but after spending time with him, I learned it was Jack's way of saying he was friendly.

I worried he would continue to display his toothy grin. If he did, people would most likely hurry past, thinking he was aggressive.

Taking the leash from around my neck, I stood up. He sat up straight, ears pricked forward with excitement, showing his teeth.

Even though I thought I was right about his display of teeth, I still had some misgivings until I had handled him.

Unlocking his kennel door, I stepped in, still talking in a low voice. He remained sitting, with his docked tail wagging back and forth. I moved around him, and he watched me, still flashing his teeth.

Suddenly, he stood and excitedly spun around. He sat

when I asked him to sit, so I took the leash from around my neck. Watching him closely, I slowly lowered it in front of him. He stretched out his neck and slipped his head through as I pulled it tight.

"Okay, smart boy," I said. "Let's go for a walk."

As we walked through the dog pods, I wondered why his owners had not told us about his propensity of showing teeth all the time. After living with him, they must have known it wasn't aggression, but I could understand why the mailman was scared of him.

As we walked through the pods, the dogs barked at him. He flashed his toothy grin at them, wagging his docked tail.

We entered the main hall and walked toward the outside door. It was beautiful outdoors, so we took a pleasant walk in the sunshine around the facility.

When we returned to my office, I knew he would lie down and relax for a while. He got on the Kuranda bed and put his head down to rest.

If I looked at him, he would look up with his ears pricked forward and give me a quick smile.

I dubbed his smile the flash.

Heather knocked on my door with his paperwork. When she walked in, he gave her his toothy smile.

"I don't trust him," she said nervously. "He's still showing teeth."

"He's smiling," I told her.

"Well, it looks aggressive to me," she said, not convinced.

"Watch," I told her.

I sat down on the floor a short distance from him, and when I looked at him, he showed his teeth. He repeated this several times while I sat there.

"He is actually friendly," I said. "He just has a habit of

showing his teeth like some people smile when they're nervous."

"I'm still not convinced, and how are we going to convince the public he is friendly when he is doing that?" She said, pointing at him.

"I don't know," I said, looking at him concerned. "It's going to be a problem."

My concerns were well-founded, and soon we were getting complaints about the aggressive dog in Kennel 12.

By now the staff and volunteers understood it was one of Jack's odd personality traits, although an unfortunate one. People hurried by his kennel and would not stop to interact with him.

This was regrettable because the Jack we had become acquainted with was friendly.

We tried to explain to visitors that it was not aggression but a friendly smile. But as time went by, we became concerned because we were not receiving any applications for him.

One staff member suggested we post a sign on the outside of Jack's kennel to explain his smile. We made the sign with big bold letters, which read,

"Jack's so friendly that he smiles at you."

This helped a little, and a few people edged close enough to read the sign. Jack would lift his head and happily display his friendly teeth.

But the public remained unconvinced, and would move away wary and unsure.

"He looks aggressive to me," people stated.

Jack seemed jinxed by a smile, and unfortunately people could not see past the pearly white teeth.

We get many volunteers at the shelter, and those who are interested in walking dogs go through training. After their training, some volunteers remained nervous around Jack.

Luckily, one volunteer named Mac seemed to understand that Jack was not aggressive. Ignoring his teeth, he started taking him out for walks.

Mac volunteered one day a week, but after meeting Jack he started coming every day because he was concerned Jack might not be taken out. He was probably right, so we welcomed his dedication with Jack.

Mac seemed to have a deviant sense of humor, and after their walk he would bring Jack through the front door. He seemed to relish the reaction people had as they were walking past the front counter.

Startled, people would move away from them. If there were children present, their parents would pull them close beside them, or pick them up as they carefully watched Jack.

If Jack realized people were looking at him, he reciprocated with his toothy grin.

How do you break a dog from showing its teeth, even if it is a cheerful grin? I have to admit it was a quandary, and I was beside myself about how to handle the situation.

Even if people understood he was not being aggressive, they seemed hesitant to take him home. They did not want to explain to their family, friends, and people in their neighborhood that Jack was not being aggressive, but was just simply smiling.

Especially the mailman, pizza delivery driver, or Amazon, who were delivering the mail, food, or packages.

Jack continued his pageantry, and we continued to try to find him a home.

He smiled his way around the shelter, and we discovered it even unnerved the dogs. When he walked past their kennels, the dogs would charge toward the front, barking.

The more timid dogs ran to their beds to look for a place to hide.

Jack seemed totally unaware of the chaos he was causing and continued to smile congenially as he walked past their kennels.

There was one nice couple who didn't seem to be put off by Jack's smiles. They felt another dog would be good company for their dog when they were away at work.

We were excited and thought this might be a perfect match.

We scheduled an appointment for the two dogs to meet. They came to the shelter on the appointed date and introduced us to their dog, Gigi, a mini Aussie.

They waited in the play yard while Heather and I went to get Jack.

As we approached them, Jack, of course, showed his choppers. Gigi was wary and immediately moved behind her owner.

Entering the play yard, Jack continued to smile and give butt wiggles as he wagged his docked tail in excitement. No matter how we tried to coax her, Gigi refused to meet Jack.

"I don't think this is going to work," the woman said, disappointed.

She picked Gigi up, trying to comfort her.

"I'm sorry, Jack," she stated sympathetically.

Jack had been on walks with other dogs, and he loved them. The other dogs were always cautious in the first meeting until they could get past Jack's silly grin.

It was very confusing to them because in their world, showing teeth is a sign of aggression, and usually a warning to stay away. They were having trouble reading Jack and did not trust his body language.

Dogs go by smell, hearing, and sight, so when a dog is showing behaviors such as Jack was, it is misleading.

His behavior confused dogs because they did not smell aggression on him, and did not hear him growl. But the showing of teeth was a sign of aggressiveness, and they had a hard time getting past his Dr. Jekyll and Mr. Hyde grin.

We moved him into the first pod, to a kennel closest to the door. That way, we would not have to hear all the hullabaloo from the other dogs when Jack walked past their kennels.

Mac continued to walk Jack, and if he met someone outdoors, he tried to promote him by explaining that it was not aggression they were seeing, but simply a smile.

People wanted to believe Mac, but Jack's display of teeth spoke volumes. They backed away with no desire to move forward and interact with him.

As Jack's stay became longer and longer, we started talking about transferring him out to another shelter. When they asked us why Jack was not being adopted, we told them about his smiles.

Even though they thought it was adorable, they turned us down because they knew they would have a hard time placing him. We reached out to other facilities with the same results.

Mac was beside himself with worry, because the longer a dog spends at the shelter, they become stressed and start displaying troublesome behaviors.

The herding breeds are notorious for becoming stir crazy in a kennel environment. As a working breed, they dislike being confined with nothing to do, and they can become very clever in how to entertain themselves.

As time dragged on, Jack became more stressed. One morning we found his bed shredded, his water bowl turned upside down, and the Kuranda bed dismantled.

Jack was barking endlessly, and even though staff members and volunteers were giving him more attention, it was not enough stimulation for him.

"Jack's going crazy!" Mac said one day.

"I know. I'm worried about him," I said sadly.

It was raining outdoors, and he had just gotten back after taking Jack outside. The rain was dripping off his raincoat, making a puddle on the floor. He wiped a drop from the end of his nose before continuing.

"I was talking with another volunteer yesterday, and he told me he would consider adopting Jack."

"Oh!" I said, encouraged. "Who is that?"

"James."

"Doesn't he live in an apartment?" I questioned.

"He does, but he goes out every afternoon or evening to plein-air paint."

I had met James, but most of the time he came on my days off. He had volunteered for a couple of years, and he was very committed to the dogs.

Quiet and easygoing, James came in twice a week to walk a few dogs, and then discreetly slipped away.

"Have him fill out an application for Jack," I told Mac.

"He has," Mac said, acting surprised that I did not know. "But the director told James she was concerned because stock dogs normally do not work out well in an apartment setting."

"Oh! I'm sorry to hear that, but isn't James retired, and isn't he home most of the time?"

Mac answered both questions with an affirmative head shake.

"I can understand why she's concerned," he said, blowing out his breath. "And I understand Jack is a working breed, but I think James would provide a wonderful home for him."

"Let me talk with her," I said, convinced I could change her mind. "Because at this point, what have we got to lose."

I went to the application drawer at the front counter and pulled out James's application on Jack.

Knocking on my director's door, I waited for her invitation for me to come in.

"Door's open," she said, rolling back her chair.

"What's up?"

I sat down across from her, ready to make my case.

"I have an application for Jack," I said.

"Well, hurrah," she said, with relief in her voice.

I handed it across her desk, and she reached out to take it from me.

"I know he's very stressed, and needs to get out of here," she said, looking at the application.

She read through it and then looked at me.

"I think I already saw this one?" She said, puzzled.

"Yes," I said. "You have, but I don't feel they explained to you who was trying to adopt Jack, and the kind of home he would give him."

She placed the application down on the desk and looked at me closely.

"Well," she responded, "tell me why you think this would be a suitable home for Jack?"

My director took animal placement very seriously, wanting each animal in the shelter to go to a home that was suitable for the breed.

I understood her thinking, but I felt this home would be perfect for Jack.

I leaned forward to explain what kind of life Jack would have with James.

"James is retired," I said. "He has time for a dog, and he is an artist who plein-air paints like my husband."

She had a confused look on her face, and I realized she might not know what plein-air painting was.

"Do you know what plein-air painting is?" I asked her.

"I guess I don't," she said, picking up her coffee cup. "Why don't you tell me."

"It means open air. He paints outdoors. Because he paints

outdoors, he would take Jack with him wherever he goes. They could be up in the mountains, out in an open field, or painting by a river. Jack will go with him, and will have a great time snooping around while James is painting. Mark loves to take our dog with him when he paints."

She leaned forward, listening.

"James has been a volunteer for over two years, and has shown great dedication," I continued. "I know he would make a great owner for Jack."

She sat quietly, reading the rest of the application.

"Well," she finally said, "I was very concerned with the apartment setting, but you have given me a better under-standing of the life Jack will have with James, so I'm willing to try this."

She picked up her pen and scribbled approved across the top of the application.

Leaning back in her chair, she smiled.

"Call James and see if he is still interested."

I went to the front counter to make the call. It rang several times before James answered.

"James," I said, when I heard his voice, "this is Julie at the Humane Society. We were looking at your application on Jack, and wondered if you are still interested in him."

There was a long pause on the other end of the line before he answered.

"I would love to," he said. "But I'm curious. What made your director change her mind? She seemed pretty adamant that Jack shouldn't live in an apartment?"

"You're right," I said. "Most of the time stock dogs don't do well in apartments, but I explained to her how much time you spend outdoors painting, and that you are retired. Now she understands Jack will be with you most of the time. Once she realized that, she changed her mind."

"I'm so glad," he said, with relief in his voice. "He will be with me all the time, so when can I come get him?"

I made arrangements so that he could come the following afternoon.

Once the adoption was completed, we waved a smiling James and smiling Jack goodbye.

A year later on a warm spring day, James walked into my husband's gallery with Jack tagging along. He shook my husband's hand and introduced him to Jack. My husband was excited to meet Jack and have a conversation about art with James.

"This must be the infamous smiler," my husband said, reaching down to pet Jack.

James laughed. "Yes, this is the legendary Smiling Jack."

James looked around the gallery, admiring Mark's work. He pointed out different paintings he liked and complimented Mark on how he captured the light in his paintings.

Mark pulled a chair over to the desk and invited James to sit down.

"My wife told me you are an artist, and I remembered meeting you at an art show once."

"Yes, but painting had become a struggle for me, and about a year ago I was ready to give it up," James said.

Mark looked at him, surprised.

James continued petting the top of Jack's head while telling his story.

"It had become very difficult to paint if people were around," he sighed. After I had found a place to paint, and would spend time setting up, I knew I only had a small amount of time to paint before the light changed. Just as the light was perfect, and I was at a crucial point in the painting, someone would walk up to look. They would look over my shoulder and try to have a conversation with me.

Some admired what I was painting, and some were critical. They would find fault with the colors, advise me to take a tree out, or put a bird right there while pointing at a spot, or suggest I place a person in a boat on the water.

Some people were so oblivious and would stand directly in front of the scene I was attempting to paint.

"I had tried several locations, but it was happening so often I finally gave it up, and stayed home."

My husband shook his head in agreement. He had experienced the same things while out painting.

James complained, "I didn't feel free to paint and not be interrupted. I decided to stay home and paint in my studio."

Then, a mischievous smile crossed his lips.

"Luckily, I adopted Jack, and he has solved all my problems."

My husband looked at him inquisitively. "How did Jack help?"

"His smiles," James laughed. "When I'm out painting, and people approach me, they will notice Jack lying beside me showing his teeth. They stop before getting too close to ask if he is friendly.

I'll wave my paintbrush around as if warning them to stay away, and yell, 'Don't come any closer.'

"They back away, and walk around us in a wide circle."

Mark laughed, and James continued his story.

"He wouldn't hurt a flea," James said. "But they don't know that, and I continue to paint without being disturbed."

"Clever," Mark said, still laughing.

James looked down at Jack.

"Poor Jack," he said. "He really is friendly, but people leave us alone thinking he will attack them any moment."

James started laughing, enjoying the hilarity of how he had solved his problem, and had found a way to paint in solitude.

"Jack's smile has given me my freedom back."

James continued coming to the gallery once or twice a year to visit Mark. Jack always laid at his feet beside him.

They had become working partners, with James happily painting, and Jack happily smiling.

They had been together for eight years when, on a cool November day, James came to the gallery without Jack.

"I got up one morning, and he was gone," James said, wiping away a tear. "He was lying on his bed and must have died during the night."

Mark called to tell me about Jack's passing.

The staff at the shelter felt bad for James. He had been a perfect match for Jack, and we knew he would be lonely without him.

James continued to come to the gallery to visit with Mark, and occasionally they would meet to plein-air paint in the evenings.

The next fall after Jack's death, Mark came home with the news that James was moving to Texas.

After his move, we received a Christmas card telling us he was well and enjoying new scenery to paint.

Cards followed for a couple of years, and then they came more sporadically.

Finally, we did not hear from James any longer.

Like so many shelters, there comes a time when expansion is needed. It is important to have room for the growing animal population caused by urban growth.

Our shelter was in one of those times with a huge influx of cats. We built a cat wing onto the shelter to house cats and pocket animals.

When it was finished, we had a grand opening, inviting the public to come and view it.

The morning of the opening, I walked through the halls of the new cat wing for the first time.

It had eight new cat rooms with outdoor patios, and at the end of the hall, two storage rooms.

People had donated to the shelter for the new wing, and some rooms had memorial plaques honoring people who had made large donations.

On the wall beside one room was a plaque with James and Jack's picture on it.

I stopped to read the plaque, and it read: In memorial to James and Jack with a donation in the amount of $20,000.00.

I stood in front of it, surprised, because I had not heard of James's passing.

"He died?" I said, stunned, turning to look at my director, who had walked up behind me.

"Yes, about a year ago," she said. "A couple of months ago, we got a call from James's lawyer, who told us he had left a donation for the shelter in his will."

"Wow!" I said. "What a gift!"

Looking again at the plaque, I felt mixed emotions. One of sadness because they were both gone, and of happiness because James and Jack had found each other.

My director patted me on the shoulder.

"Smiling Jack," I replied, reminiscing.

In the picture, they were sitting together on a mountain, looking down a valley. James had his arm over Jack's back.

I stood looking at James and Jack's picture thinking about how Jack's adoption almost didn't take place. What a perfect match they had been for each other.

James had looked beyond Jack's flashing teeth to see the loyal dog he was.

What a gift Jack had been for him, and James reciprocated with a gift to the Humane Society.

It had come full circle.

With his gift, it helped build a new wing onto the shelter, and we were able to help other animals find new homes.

That is worth smiling about.

My dog is not just a pet, he's a source of endless entertainment.

UNKNOWN

MAPLE

"This is Maple," the elderly gentleman said, looking through his thick glasses at me. "I can't keep her any longer."

Before me stood a very old dog. Swayed back with age, her muzzle was graying, and she looked at me with weary eyes that were intelligent and kind. Her coat was light brown with a splash of white on her chest between her front legs.

"How old is she?" I asked.

"At least fourteen," he commented, patting her gently on the head as she slowly swished her tail back and forth.

"It looks like she has had good care, Mr?" I held out my hand toward him.

His hand appeared from beneath the frayed coat sleeve to gently shake my hand.

"Greer," he said, telling me his last name.

"Mr. Greer," I said. "It is nice to meet you. My name is Julie, and this is Heather."

We escorted Mr. Greer into an office, and Maple followed close behind him.

"Please sit down," Heather said, pulling a chair out.

He lowered his thin, aging body slowly onto the chair, and then leaned forward so he could hear better.

"She's a fine girl, she is," he said, looking at his dog affectionately. "I've had her since she were a pup."

I sat across from him, looking at his rumpled clothing and aged, calloused hands as he tenderly petted his dog with fondness.

"She was a grand lass, she were, won ribbons in the county fair for her beauty."

Maple licked his hands affectionately as she tried to see him through her fading, opaque eyes.

"Mr. Greer, is there a reason you are trying to bring your dog to the shelter today?" I questioned him.

His eyes brimmed with tears, and he looked earnestly at me.

"I don't want to, but I'm dying," he stated.

The room went silent, and Heather and I sat stunned as we tried to sort out in our minds what this kindhearted man was saying.

"You mean you want to bring her into the shelter because you're dying?" I questioned.

Suddenly, tears rolled down his wrinkled cheeks, and they dropped onto his worn overalls. His gnarled hand reached into a pocket, pulling out a hanky so he could wipe the tears away.

"I'm afraid I will die, and my lass will be in the house alone with no one to care for her," he said, with earnestness in his voice. "So if you could find a home for her, I know she would be safe."

Bewildered, I sat back in my chair and looked at Heather, wondering what she was thinking. She looked back at me with sad eyes, unsure if she had heard correctly what Mr. Greer was telling us.

"Mr. Greer, don't you have family who can look in on you, and take Maple when you are gone?" she asked.

"Na, no none," he replied sadly, wiping his nose with the hanky. "Everyone is gone."

"Do you have a close neighbor or friend?" she further inquired.

"Neighbors, yes, but they don't check on me often. They all have very busy lives, and at my age all my friends are gone."

Again, Heather and I looked at each other. It was evident this man was all alone in the world, and he was frightened of what would become of Maple if he died. Without saying anything to each other, we knew we had to find a way so he could keep his dog.

Aging pets do come to the Humane Society. People bring in their old, geriatric dogs or cats and ask for them to be adopted out, or some owners ask for them to be euthanized. We instruct them how hard it will be to find a home for an older pet, but we will take them if the owner insists.

Regarding euthanasia, we provide counseling, advising them to take their pets to a veterinarian to be humanely euthanized if that is what they want to do. It is overwhelming for owners to make an end-of-life decision, and some people feel as if they are betraying their beloved pet. This is heartbreaking for both the pet and its owners, who have loved it. After we talk with them, they usually do the right thing for their pets. We have found they just need to hear it is okay to let their pets go.

Senior dogs are kind and gentle beings, plodding slowly through their remaining years, months, weeks, or days that they have left. After years of loyalty and love, they are trusting their owners to care for them in their old age.

We are heartbroken when older pets are abandoned or relinquished into our care. If we cannot find a new home for them, they will die at the shelter in an unfamiliar place. Even though we try to love them in their final moments, we are not their beloved owners. So when the moment comes, we will sit next to them with their head in our lap, gently petting them. Holding them, we try to bring comfort in their last moments as they complete the life cycle.

With Mr. Greer sitting across from us, we knew we had to find a better solution so he and Maple would not be separated. I excused myself and walked across the hall to my director's office. Knocking on her open door, I waited for an invitation to come in. She was behind her desk working on her computer and waved me in. She put her glasses on top of a stack of papers and smiled.

"What's up?" she asked, grabbing her coffee cup, which most likely was cold by now.

I sat down across from her and told her about the situation with Mr. Greer and Maple.

"What should we do?" I asked, hoping she would bring some of her wisdom and experience to the situation.

"Well, we are not taking that dog and separating those two," she answered adamantly.

"Give me a minute, and I'll come over and talk with him."

She waved me off as she turned toward her file cabinet, opening a drawer. I left her office and walked back across the hall to where Mr. Greer was sitting with Heather.

"Our director will be in to visit with you in a few minutes," I told him.

When she entered the office, she reached out to shake Mr. Greer's hand, and looking down at Maple, she asked,

"And who is this?"

"This is my Maple. She is the love of my life," he said with fondness.

"Hello, Maple," our director said, gently extending her hand to touch the top of Maple's head.

Pulling a chair out, she sat down next to Mr. Greer, tapping him on the knee.

"Mr. Greer, I think Maple needs to stay with you, and I am determined to find a way for that to happen."

Mr. Greer's shoulders started to shake, and he threw his hands over his face to hide his tears.

"I don't see how you can. I am a very sick man, and I don't have a lot of time left."

Our director sat quietly with him until he could control his emotions. Reaching out, she took his hand in hers.

"Well, we have our ways. Give me twenty-four hours, and I'll come up with a plan for you and Maple, okay?"

His shoulders shook with emotion, and again he lifted his hands to his face. Maple knew he was upset and leaned closer to him, laying her head on his lap. With trembling hands he reached out for her, tenderly rubbing her soft ears.

"Thank you," he whispered, wiping tears from his eyes.

"Come back tomorrow," our director said, trying to reassure him with an encouraging smile.

"By then we should have a plan for you and Maple. Can you trust us with this?"

"Yes, I'll try," he said, with some hope in his eyes. "It will be such a relief to know my Maple is safe and taken care of."

He thanked us and leaned down to pick up Maple's leash. Two weary souls, they slowly walked toward the front doors. After his car had left the parking lot, Heather and I turned at the same time to look at our director.

"What are we going to do?" I asked.

"We are going to get to work and find some answers for this poor man and his dog," she said. "I'm determined those two will remain together until one of them passes."

Walking toward her office, she looked back when she reached the door.

"Heather, look up the number for Old Dog Haven. I want to talk with them. And Julie, find the number for our local hospice. I am interested in how they handle patients with dogs."

She entered her office, and before she sat down, we heard,

"Come on, girls, let's get moving. I need those numbers so we will have a plan for Mr. Greer and Maple by tomorrow."

Looking up numbers, we started placing calls to gather information and resources. At the end of the day, we had a plan. Everything was in place, and we were ready for Mr. Greer when he arrived the next day.

Before Mr. Greer came to the shelter the next morning, we had a folder ready with all the information on hospice care for people with pets, and a plan with Old Dog Haven.

Old Dog Haven told us they had some openings, and our director had talked with one of the potential fosters who would be willing to take Maple. They told our director they would keep their home open so Maple could come to them if Mr. Greer died before her.

At 1:00, Mr. Greer's car drove onto the shelter property. Carefully, he emerged from his car, and Maple slowly followed him. They took their time walking up the sidewalk and into the building. Heather escorted them to the same office they had been in on the previous day.

"How are you doing, Mr. Greer?" She asked, trying to keep the conversation light.

"Well, I didn't sleep very well last night," he said wearily. "I was in a lot of pain, and uncertain what would happen today."

"I'm so sorry," Heather responded. "But I think today will be a better day for you and Maple."

"I hope so, but you know, you can't turn back time," he said, with a far-off look. "But I have wonderful memories with my Maple."

"I know you do, and we are hoping you will have more," Heather said, smiling.

Heather notified our director that Mr. Greer had arrived. When she came into the office, she had the file in her hand. Sitting down next to Mr. Greer, she patted him on his arm.

"Mr. Greer," she said, "I think we have some good news for you."

Spreading the papers out in front of him, she pointed at each one. He reached into his front pocket for his glasses and positioned them on his nose. Picking up the first paper, he slowly and methodically began to read. After he had read each paper, he placed them down on the desktop. Pulling the glasses off his face, he looked closely at our director with both relief and uncertainty.

"What does this exactly mean?" he said, tapping on the papers with his arthritic finger.

"It means if you agree, you can keep Maple," she told him.

He sat quietly before speaking, then in a voice tight with emotion, he said,

"But you don't understand. I'm dying. I'm terminally ill."

"I understand," our director said, turning her chair so she could face him. She took both his hands in hers.

"You need to keep Maple, not only for your sake, but for hers. If you pass before her, we have made arrangements for Maple to go to a foster home with Old Dog Haven. They are a wonderful organization that will keep her until she passes. She will be safe, loved, and well taken care of. When it is time for her life to end on this earth, she will die in the loving arms of her foster family." She patted him on the knee. "Do you understand what I am trying to tell you?"

He nodded his head up and down as big tears rolled down his cheeks.

"You need Maple, and she needs you."

She grabbed a box of tissues, holding it in front of him so he could take one.

"Are you still living in your home?" she questioned him.

"Yes. They told me hospice will start coming in when the time comes, and I need them."

Our director picked up one of the papers lying on the desk.

"A nurse at hospice told me you will be able to keep Maple at home with you," she said.

He shook his head with a concerned look.

"Yes, I know that, but what frightens me is what would happen if I pass before hospice is called in. Then Maple would be alone with me before I'm found," he said, distressed.

Placing the paper back down on the desk, our director took his hands back in hers.

"I thought that was what you were worried about, Mr. Greer. So we have made arrangements to prevent that from happening. Myself, or one of my staff will call you twice a day. Once in the morning, and then again before we leave the shelter at the end of the day. I have also made arrangements for Meals on Wheels to deliver meals to you once a day. On the weekends when they will not be coming in, my church will bring in meals for you. That way, someone is checking on you at least three times a day. Once hospice comes, we will stop, unless you need us."

Mr. Greer covered his face and sobbed. Our director sat quietly with him until he could regain his composure.

"I can't believe how kind you are," he said, and for the first time there was a slight smile. "I am so grateful."

"We want what is best for you and Maple," our director reassured him. "We have also made arrangements with the fosters from Old Dog Haven, and if it is okay with you, they would like to come and meet Maple. They are also willing to come to your home a couple of times each week to take Maple for a walk. That way they will not be strangers to her if you pass before her."

He reached down and held Maple's head in his hands.

"Do you hear what these nice ladies have done for us, Maple?" he said, with relief in his voice.

When it was time for Mr. Greer and Maple to leave, our director walked with them to their car. Two elderly souls, they were now ghosts of who they had once been. Their bodies were betraying them, and now they faced the reality of dying. He opened the back door and carefully helped Maple in. Turning, he gave our director a hug. He opened the front door of his car, and before he got in, he waved to Heather and me. We waved back, feeling such relief because we knew Mr. Greer and Maple would remain together.

Over the next three months, we made our morning and evening calls to Mr. Greer. With each call we could hear a more weakened voice, and knew his was failing. Then on a sunny spring day, hospice notified us, informing us Mr. Greer was now in their care.

We still called, because he had become a loved friend, and talking with him had become a pleasant part of each of our days. As weak as he was, we looked forward to hearing Mr. Greer's pleasant, gravelly voice.

"Maple is lying beside me on the bed," he would say each time. "She's a grand lass."

One morning when we called, the phone rang and rang. Concerned, we placed a call to hospice. Later in the morning, they returned our call to tell us Mr. Greer had passed.

We stood at the front desk and cried. We cried for this charming, kind man, who loved his dog and had to leave her behind, and for Maple, who was left behind. Devoted and loyal, she remained beside him until the end.

True to her promise, our director called Old Dog Haven

and made arrangements for the fosters to come pick up Maple at the shelter. Heather drove to Mr. Greer's house to pick her up, and when they arrived back, we placed her in our director's office with her soft bed from home. We could tell she was bewildered by the worry lines on her face, and we tried to comfort her.

Shelly and Tom, the foster parents, arrived early afternoon to pick her up. They had been fosters for Old Dog Haven for over ten years. A wonderful couple, they had welcomed many senior dogs into their home, giving love and comfort until they passed. Because they had been going to Mr. Greer's home to walk Maple, she already knew them. Before they left, they promised they would keep us informed about how Maple was doing.

Once a month, either Shelly or Tom would call to tell us how Maple was. At other times, Shelly would bring Maple to the shelter to see us. The last time she brought her in, Maple's face had turned completely white, and she walked slower because her legs had become more feeble. I don't think she could see at all by now, but she was still friendly and managed a slight tail wag. We could see her body was very weak and was now failing her, and we knew her time was nearing. Heather and I got down on the floor in front of her to snuggle and love on her. Before they left, I placed her head in my hands, as Mr. Greer used to do, and said to her,

"You're a grand lass."

Wagging her tail, she quietly seemed to accept the inevitable. Perhaps she was happy, because she knew she would once again be with her beloved Mr. Greer.

We did not hear from Shelly for a couple of weeks. Then, early one summer morning, we got a call from Tom, telling us that Maple had passed.

We had mixed emotions. We were sad, but also we felt

comforted because Maple had been released from her weak-ened body and was once again with her beloved friend, Mr. Greer.

"Why is that?" Heather asked, sighing as she wiped away tears. "Why do I feel both sadness and relief?"

Our director patted her on the shoulder sympathetically.

"We feel sad because of loss. It's hard to watch animals or people suffer, but we feel relief and a kind of joy, because two loving souls who were separated for a time are now back together."

She grabbed a box of tissues, passing them around.

"Because we work at a shelter, we are continually in a state of exhilaration and happiness, or we are in a state of sorrow and grief. It is what we witness here, and that makes people like you so special. It is because you care, and are willing to help the helpless."

We all smiled at her as we wiped tears.

"At least we kept them together as long as we could, and I think that was a job well done," I added.

"Yes, well done, my friends," our director said, smiling as she wiped away a tear. "Well done."

The bond between a pet and a human is a sacred one, and when a pet is gone, a part of us goes with them.

JAMES HERRIOT

I Call You Dog

*When God made the earth and sky, flowers and the trees, He
then made all the animals, the birds and the bees.*

When his work was finished, not one was quite the same.

He said, "I'll walk this earth of mine and give you all a name.

*And so he traveled land and sea, and everywhere he went. A
little creature followed him until his strength was spent.*

*When all were named upon the earth and in the sky and sea, the
little creature said, "Dear Lord, there's not one left for me."*

*The Father smiled and softly said, "I've left You till the end, I'll
turn my own name back to front, and call you dog, my friend."*

AUTHOR UNKNOWN

ACKNOWLEDGEMENTS

To Janine, Erika, Tiffany, Annie, Eileen, Jane, Jarin, Kim, Christina, Veronica, my co-workers, and so many, many others who devote their lives and hearts to animals, and work so hard to make the animals in their care better.

To many beloved volunteers, Cindy, Lucy, John, Debbie, Debra, Jannet, Mackenzie, Dianna, David, and so many, many more who give hours and hours of their time walking or caring for dogs, and all animals at the shelter. Your hearts are huge.

To all the beautiful people I met, who were willing to adopt a dog, bring them into their homes, and give them a second chance.

To the Veterinarians, Vet Techs, and their staff, who work tirelessly for the care of shelter animals.

To Animal Control Officers, and Police Officers who are the first ones on the line, witnessing horrible situations that animals have to suffer.

To the Northwest Battle Buddies, who provide trained service dogs to Vererans battling PTSD.

To our Veterans, and all men and woman who serve our country, thank you.

To our Senior Citizens, who enjoy the company of a dog.

My Husband, for listening to my writing, encouraging me to write.

My Mom Georgia, Children Kim, Melynda and Lance, Sister Linda and Brother David their support and love.

Thank you Marion, from Seaport Books, for you great advise and encouragement.

To my Editor Julie Pershing, for your hard work, and knowledge, a big thank you.

ABOUT THE AUTHOR

Julie Bistranin was raised in the Shields Valley of rural Montana. Surrounding herself with animals, she easily joined their natural world. Her grandfather taught her that animals were teachers, and we journey through life with them. He had a special gift with horses, passing down this gift to Julie, but her passion was with dogs. Their behaviors, pack mentality, loyalty, and natural inclination to please drew her in, making them easy to train. She studied dogs to understand their thinking and the characteristics of different breeds, so she could train them to reach their full inherent potential.

After moving to Washington, she served fifteen years working at her local animal shelter, where she focused on evaluating, correcting behavior problems, and training. Helping dogs become better behaved, find loving homes, or be placed in suitable working situations was a source of great honor for Julie. Since retiring, she dedicates her time to writing and lives in Mt Vernon, Washington, with her husband, Mark.

How You Can Help: Leave a Review!

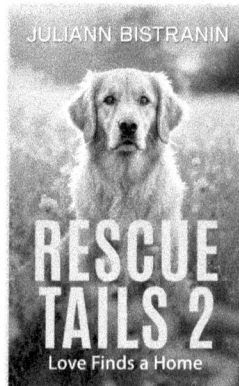

If you enjoyed *Rescue Tails 2: Love Finds a Home*, I would be so grateful if you would take a moment to leave a positive review on Amazon.

Your feedback, even a few words, helps other readers discover these stories and supports independently published books like this one.

Thank you for being part of this journey. 🐾

Rescue Tails:

Unbreakable Bonds Between Dogs & Humans

Rescue Tails: Unbreakable Bonds Between Dogs & Humans invites you into a world of resilience, second chances, and the life-changing impact of love between humans and their four-legged friends.

This collection of heartfelt stories showcases the transformative power of compassion, celebrating the remarkable journeys of dogs who've overcome past hardships to embrace a future filled with trust and unwavering companionship.

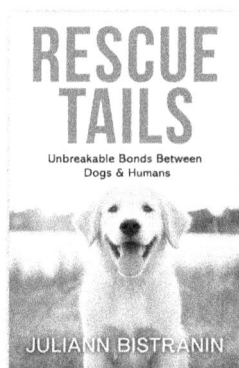

RESCUE TAILS

Unbreakable Bonds Between
Dogs & Humans

JULIANN BISTRANIN

Your Journey Begins Here...

Turn Your Passion into a Published Book

Bring your book to life—connect with us today!

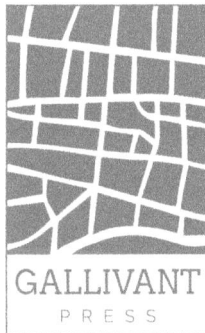

www.ingramcontent.com/pod-product-compliance
Lightning Source LLC
Chambersburg PA
CBHW062121020426
42335CB00013B/1051